Connecting Soul, Spirit, Mind, and Body

Connecting
Soul, Spirit, Mind, and Body

A Collection of Spiritual
and Religious Perspectives and
Practices in Counseling

Edited by
Ryan D. Foster
Janice Miner Holden

AQUILINE BOOKS I **UNT**
An Imprint of the University of North Texas Libraries
Denton

Published by
University of North Texas Libraries
1155 Union Circle #305190
Denton, TX 76203–5017

ISBN: 978-1-68040-008-3
DOI: http://dx.doi.org/10.12794/sps.connecting-008-3

Cover design: Gail Kerrigan

Table of Contents

Foreword

Craig Cashwell, Janice Miner Holden,
and Lisa Jackson-Cherry

Craig Cashwell

Soon after my year of service as ASERVIC President, I (Craig) had the idea that practicing counselors needed a simple guide to spiritual practices to broaden their understanding of the range of spiritual experiences that clients might bring into the counseling process and of practices that counselors might have at their disposal as an adjunct to the talk therapy process. At the time, ASERVIC was still working to establish itself as an organization that championed diversity of beliefs and practices, and I thought this project would promote that notion as well.

I consulted with those in my inner circle and began to solicit brief manuscripts on various spiritual practices. I wanted to include among the authors both academics and practitioners. The intention was that these briefs would provide a simple and concise introduction to a range of spiritual practices, with recommended readings and brief reference lists to support further exploration, should the reader so desire.

The manuscripts began to come in, and I started the editing process . . . and an odd thing happened. While I remained convinced that this was a worthwhile project, I lost my focus and, in a fairly short time, my energy around the project. It became clear to me that, without help, the project would, as the saying goes, "die on the vine."

Gaining clarity that I was not the person to push this project to the finish, I began to talk to other ASERVIC leaders about the project. Enter Dr. Jan Holden of the University of North Texas, who expressed an interest in the project. I sent her all of the manuscripts in their current form along with my gratitude for her willingness to pick up the project where I had left it.

Jan Holden

At the time that I received the manuscripts from Craig, I (Jan) had every intention of bringing the project to completion; I didn't realize it would become a relay event in which I was receiving a baton I'd be passing along to yet another editor. At the time, then–graduate assistant (now Dr.) Leslie Burwell-Pender was working with me. Together we expanded the list of topics for what we thought would become a book, communicated with potential authors, received additional manuscripts, and made further edits.

Another step we took was to submit a book proposal to the American Counseling Association. The primary point in the ACA reviewers' feedback was their request for documentation of the evidence base for the practices described in each of the manuscripts. Because research on most of these practices ranges from sparse to nonexistent, Leslie and I thought that ACA's requirements and ASERVIC's vision for the book seemed irreconcilably different. Before we could regroup to consider other possible publishers, Leslie graduated and moved away. At the time, I didn't have another graduate assistant whose professional interests fit with this project—and, like Craig before me, I lost focus and commitment.

When the ASERVIC Board inquired about the status of the project, we agreed that I would turn it back to them to decide if and how to proceed. I notified the then–approximately 35 actual or potential authors of the project's progress and developments and passed the baton, delivering all materials into Lisa Jackson-Cherry's competent hands.

Lisa Jackson-Cherry

The monograph project was on the radar of several ASERVIC presidents who preceded me (Lisa). During my first leadership role as secretary under Dr. Tracey Robert, Dr. Cheri Smith, and Dr. Mike Robinson, I was tasked with finding what had become lost monographs. Without their drive to locate the monographs, this project might still be in hibernation. The problem was that we had no idea where they were located. However, we had key individuals to start the monograph hunt, and eventually the key persons were located. The project would remain in stealth mode for a couple more years.

Then, during my terms as president-elect and president, the leadership team decided to focus on the needs of our members. We hosted a focus group during the first ASERVIC National Conference in Lake Junaluska, North Carolina, to gather this information. Following the conference, some invited past leaders (many from ASERVIC's first Summit on Spirituality in 1995) and current leadership stayed a couple of extra days to review the information gathered from the focus group and to plan ASERVIC's future initiatives. The final strategic plan (developed now under Summit II) included revising the Nine Spiritual and Religious Competencies (developed by Summit I leaders), planning additional national conferences and on-line publications of spiritual and religious teaching modules for counselor educators . . . and revisiting the monograph project.

With the other initiatives being completed or in progress, and shortly after Dr. Ryan Foster joined the faculty at Marymount University, I asked if he would be interested in taking over the *final* item on our strategic planning list: the spiritual and religious monograph project. I (somewhat eagerly) forwarded to him all the monographs I had collected from Dr. Cashwell, Dr. Holden, and the many contributing authors. It is often interesting how things come full circle. When Ryan Foster had been a doctoral student, his major professor was Jan Holden.

I extend much appreciation to all of those who submitted chapters, who waited patiently while their papers were being located, and who fostered this project to its fullness. A special thanks to Ryan Foster, who revitalized and has completed the monograph project—rejoined in the end by Jan Holden. This collection is a great contribution to ASERVIC and to the counseling profession.

Connecting Soul, Spirit, Mind, and Body

Introduction

In a world that is increasingly diverse in many ways, including spiritually, it is incumbent upon counselors to be religiously and spiritually competent. The ASERVIC Spiritual Competencies (http://www.aservic .org/resources/spiritual-competencies/) provide guidance, especially as they have been elaborated by the contributors to Craig Cashwell and Scott Young's second edition of *Integrating Spirituality and Religion into Counseling: A Guide to Competent Practice* (http://www.counseling .org/Publications/FrontMatter/72906-FM.PDF). Although that volume includes attention to some counseling practices and alternative perspectives, space constraints precluded thorough treatment of those topics. The purpose of this collection of chapters is to contribute to a more thorough consideration.

In this volume, the chapters are organized alphabetically by topic. Within each chapter, the author(s) have usually discussed the history and theory of the topic, how to apply it in counseling, empirical research on it, and indications and contraindications for its use. Each monograph concludes with print and/or online "Suggested Resources" and a "References" section; if a source that was cited in the text of the monograph appears in the suggested resources, it is not duplicated in the references. Throughout the document, URLs and email addresses are hyperlinked; pointing one's cursor on the URL and clicking will open the Web location or blank email, respectively. Information about the editors and authors appears at the end of the collection.

The original vision for this collection was to provide a quick yet authoritative source for counselors seeking information about both well-known and not-so-well-known topics related to spirituality and religion in counseling. It is the hope of everyone involved over the years in making this publication available that it serves as a valuable resource to those who use it, helping counselors to enhance their competence in assisting clients to achieve their psychospiritual potential.

Ryan D. Foster
Janice Miner Holden

After-Death Communication

Janice Miner Holden

*I guess it's the scientist in me wanting to challenge the scientists—
set the cat amongst the pigeons. Now come on people, we have to
think about these things ... they're real and people report them and
experience them, and telling them they're hallucinating is really
quite insulting, hallucinations being a negative word . . . what
am I trying to say? I can't think of the expression, raising the flag
for widows, for young widows, and for bereaved people; yes, give
them a voice . . . bereaved people get punished enough—isolated
and so forth. No, enough.*

—Jayne, psychologist and bereavement specialist, commenting
in the aftermath of after-death communications with her
deceased husband, Robert (Knight, 2011, p. 172)

After-death communication (ADC) is an experience in which a living
person has a sense of direct contact with a deceased person (Streit-
Horn, 2011a); people also have reported contact with deceased pets.
Though ADC is essentially a spontaneous phenomenon, it can often be
facilitated through the psychotherapeutic technique of Induced After-
Death Communication (IADC; Botkin, 2000, 2005). People throughout history and across cultures have reported ADC; among the earliest
recorded was that of Roman statesman and author Marcus Tullius
Cicero, circa 45 BC (Guggenheim & Guggenheim, 1996).

Research on ADC

In 2011(a), Jenny Streit-Horn published a systematic review of all
research on ADC. She found 35 research studies published between
1894 and 2006 involving a total of over 50,000 research participants
from 24 countries. She ranked the studies by methodological quality

and then used the methodologically best studies to arrive at answers to fundamental questions about ADC.

Streit-Horn (2011a) found that at least one in three people have reported experiencing ADC some time in their lives and that ADC takes any of a number of forms. These experiences occur to people awake and asleep and to people ranging from being completely physically healthy to being on their deathbeds. Various types of ADC include those that involve a distinct sense of presence of the deceased without specific sensory phenomena; a physical sensation or mental imagery that is visual, auditory, tactile, and/or olfactory; a form of technology such as the radio, computer, or telephone; and a symbolic representation such as unusual appearances of butterflies, atypical flower bloomings, or the independent movement of physical objects. Streit-Horn (2011a) observed that most common may be dream ADC—better termed "sleep ADC," because experiencers (ADCrs) differentiate these experiences from dreams, typically saying that the experience was real or was more real than typical dreams and that whereas memory of dreams typically evaporates quickly, memory of ADCs is indelibly etched in their minds and does not degrade with time.

Streit-Horn (2011a) found that although non-bereaved people report ADC, bereaved people report it more: about 75% of people within a year of the death of a loved one, tending to decrease as time passes following the death, though some ADC occurs decades later. Both sexes report ADC but women outnumber men. People of all ages report ADC, perhaps older people slightly more—probably because they are more likely to experience deaths of people to whom they are emotionally attached. People of all nationalities report ADC, with relatively more reports from cultures in which the phenomenon is acknowledged, accepted, and affirmed. People of all ethnicities report ADC, with some reporting slightly more than others. People of all education and income levels report ADC, with low-income people possibly reporting them slightly more. People of all religious affiliations and practices and of all physical and mental conditions report ADC. Of particular relevance to health professionals, Streit-Horn found that "the great majority of ADC researchers have noted that ADCrs in their studies were mentally healthy. There is no evidence that ADC alone indicates psychological disorder or mental illness" (2011b, p. 1).

Streit-Horn (2011b) observed that

people usually find ADC to be beneficial, using descriptive words like pleasant, positive, mystical, serene, elating, helpful, comforting, healing, spiritual, and a good experience. Most ADCrs report that, as a result of the ADC, they feel reassured and comforted that the deceased continues to exist—and in a state of wellbeing and happiness, and the relational bond of love between the ADCr and the deceased continues—albeit in a different form. In summary, the ADCr feels affirmed that neither the deceased nor the relationship with the deceased has ceased; rather, both have transformed and continue. (pp. 1–2)

Streit-Horn (2011a) found that only relatively rarely have people reported distress related to ADC. When they did, the distress was almost never from the contents or experience of the ADC itself but rather was almost always from fear and/or confusion resulting from an absence of information or the presence of misinformation about ADC. Another source of distress is when ADC contradicts the ADCr's fundamental belief system.

Many of Streit-Horn's (2011a) findings were corroborated by Michele Knight (2011), who conducted a qualitative study involving multiple in-depth interviews with 21 Australian adults ("co-researchers") who had experienced ADC during bereavement. Knight (2011) observed an additional form of ADC: communication through other individuals (mediumship, channeling). Five of her co-researchers reported that other family members besides themselves had also experienced ADC with the same deceased person. Knight (2011) noted that some co-researchers had only one ADC, whereas others had multiple experiences. She found no discernable pattern of timing but a theme that the ADC occurred at a time when the experiencer was in emotional need. Among her sample, co-researchers unanimously affirmed the veracity of their experiences, and "all experiences conveyed or eventuated in something positive, reassuring, and affirming" (p. 283). As a result of the ADC, "the relationship each co-researcher experienced with the deceased [was] confirmed and/or transformed" (p. 277) in the direction of being "richer and more meaningful" (p. 277). The ADCs had "sustained [co-researchers] in ways they had not thought possible or even imagined" (p. 277). Co-researchers cited not only psychological and spiritual benefits but also intellectual ones, in that they perceived they were being educated about life and death (p. 288).

As both Knight (2011) and Streit-Horn (2011a) found, most ADCrs are adamant that their experiences were real rather than hallucinatory, even when ADC contradicted their worldviews. Beyond experiencers' subjective insistence, some authors have presented veridical cases—those in which information from the ADC could not be attributed to physical sources and was objectively verified (Guggenheim & Guggenheim, 1996; Holden, 2012).

Despite the essentially beneficial nature of ADC itself, Knight's (2011) co-researchers reported responses to disclosure of their ADCs that ranged from very negative (discounting, failing to acknowledge its psychospiritual significance) to very positive ("wonder, awe, excitement, acceptance, and unconditional support" [p. 308]), and co-researchers reported various degrees of caution and reluctance to disclose the experience to others—ranging from family members to mental health professionals. Knight (2011) found that co-researchers' ADCs invariably affected their worldviews: Those already familiar with non-material phenomena and believing in post-mortem existence assimilated the experiences and found them affirming; those unfamiliar accommodated their worldviews to include these new realities (p. 316). Knight (2011) found that co-researchers' understandings of their ADCs continued to evolve, even through their participation in her study.

Indications for Addressing ADC in Counseling

Client Report of Spontaneous ADC

Probably the most likely scenario in counseling is that a client reports a spontaneous ADC that occurred outside of session and wishes to discuss it. In such a case, counselors can adapt guidelines that mental health professionals have established for working with client near-death experiencers (NDErs; Foster, James, & Holden, 2009, pp. 255–256):

- Prepare for such disclosures by exploring one's own attitudes toward ADC and addressing any attitudes that have the potential to impair a therapeutic relationship or therapeutic procedures with an ADCr client.
- Avoid forcing one's own values on ADCr clients; rather, work with clients to explore, and evolve through intersubjective discourse, the interface between clients' ADCs and their values.

- Show respect for the potentially profound nature of ADCs and the individuality of each ADCr.
- In acknowledgement of the extensive research that ADCs are not inherently related to mental disorder, avoid labeling ADCs and ADCrs with pathological diagnoses on the basis of the ADC alone.
- Support ADCr clients in the expression of emotions surrounding the ADC and related events and in the discovery and development of the meaning of the ADC in the context of clients' worldviews.

Regarding clients' worldviews, counselors are likely best prepared to serve their clients well who realize that clients whose worldviews do not include transpersonal phenomena—those that transcend the usual personal limits of space and/or time—or the survival of consciousness after death will likely experience conflict between the veracity of their ADCs and the schemas of their worldviews. In such cases, counselors should likely be prepared to expect that clients will want to process reconciliation of the conflicting phenomena.

On a related note, because of Streit-Horn's (2011a) finding that ADC-related distress was almost always due to inadequate information or misinformation, counselors probably serve clients well by educating them about the experience: normalizing it as something reported by at least a third of people worldwide, clarifying that it is unrelated to mental disorder, and reporting its very predominantly beneficial effect or potential. To assist counselors in this process, Streit-Horn (2011b) designed a one-sheet (two-sided) ADC Fact Sheet primarily for health professionals to provide to ADCr clients. The sheet includes a summary of her findings with recommended print and online resources for clients to pursue further information. This resource is available for free download from the Internet with copyright permission for anyone to use it for health or educational purposes.

As in the case of counseling NDErs, the above guidelines are unproven in their effectiveness in counseling ADCr clients. However, extensive research indicates that ADCs almost always either immediately or eventually result in healing and enhancement of ADCrs' well-being, so a seemingly safe overall principle is to pursue in counseling whatever process unlocks the healing/enhancing potential of the ADC while working within the limits of ethicality, legality, and the client's value system.

Induced After-Death Communication

In IADC, a counselor trained in eye movement desensitization and reprocessing (EMDR) and in specific IADC procedures facilitates for the client a state of consciousness characterized by equanimity, receptivity, and benign intention that may facilitate an internal experience of communication with a deceased person to whom the client is emotionally attached (Botkin, 2005). Psychologist Allan Botkin, who developed the technique, and his colleagues have reported that, based on their own clinical observation, at least 70% of IADC clients report an ADC from the procedure (Botkin & Hannah, 2013). Furthermore, based on observations by both Botkin and 15 therapists he had trained, these experiences typically are profoundly meaningful for clients and have a beneficial effect on their grief symptoms (Hannah, Botkin, Marrone, & Streit-Horn, 2013).

Botkin's (2005) guidelines are to work with clients whose loved one died at least six months prior; as grief tends to decrease and emotional equanimity to increase with time following the death, Botkin has found that the longer the time since the death, the more likely the client is to be successful in IADC (A. Botkin, personal communication, May 21, 2013). Clients do not need to believe in the survival of consciousness after death or in the technique; in fact, Botkin has found that clients who express uncertainty or skepticism that the technique will result in an ADC are actually *more* likely to experience ADC—probably because, again, their attitude corresponds to an absence of emotional investment in having an ADC, a condition that aligns with the equanimity and passive volition Botkin has found to be critical to success (A. Botkin, personal communication, 2004).

As of the time of this publication, IADC has not yet been researched through randomized, controlled studies. Thus, it fits the American Counseling Association's ethical designation as a "developing or innovative [technique/procedure/modality]" (American Counseling Association, 2014, p. 10, standard C.7.a.), which requires counselors to exercise relevant ethical practice, such as informing clients of that designation.

Contraindications

Regarding spontaneous ADC, assuming a counselor is knowledgeable about ADC and possesses the attitudes described above, addressing these experiences in counseling is contraindicated in only a few cases. These cases include those where the client has a mental disorder that involves poor ego functioning and impairment of contact with consensus reality, if addressing ADC violates the client's fundamental beliefs and values, and if addressing ADC results in extreme emotional distress for the client. In the latter case, further intervention may reduce distress that enables further focus on the ADC.

Regarding IADC, the primary contraindication is serious chronic mental illness that, again, impairs contact with consensus reality (A. Botkin, personal communication, 2004). Botkin indicated that clients with bipolar disorder and with depression who are using medication effective in regulating symptoms can benefit from IADC. He warned that anti-anxiety medication and depression can blunt the effectiveness of EMDR (A. Botkin, personal communication, 2004).

Conclusion

Counselors who are not competent to address ADC can refer clients to those who are. One such referral source is the American Center for the Integration of Spiritually Transformative Experiences (ACISTE), which certifies mental health professionals to work with clients who have had transpersonal experiences like ADC (www.aciste.org).

Counselors who are competent to address ADC do well to inform clients of that competence in their professional disclosure statements. Considering the high incidence of ADC during bereavement, they also do well to inform their bereaved clients that, though not universal, it is not unusual for the bereaved to experience ADC and to ask such clients directly whether they have had such an experience. When clients reveal ADC, counselors do well to follow guidelines for responding therapeutically to such disclosure (Holden, 2015).

Suggested Resources

Online

Allan Botkin's IADC website: http://www.induced-adc.com/. Counselors interested in acquiring training in IADC can contact Botkin via his website.

Holden, J. M. (2015). *Responding to near-death experiences and other potentially spiritually transformative experiences: Recommendations for healthcare professionals* [PDF document]. Retrieved from http://www.coe.unt.edu/sites/default/files/22/129/14_NDE_Acronym_Handout.pdf

Streit-Horn, J. (2011b). *Fact sheet: After-death communication* [PDF document]. Retrieved from http://www.coe.unt.edu/sites/default/files/22/129/ADC.pdf. A valuable and essential resource both for the information it provides and for its inclusion of recommended print and online resources for clients to learn more about ADC; it is available for download without permission for use in education and healthcare.

References

American Counseling Association. (2014). *Code of ethics.* Alexandria, VA: Author.

Botkin, A. L. (2000). The induction of after-death communications utilizing eye-movement desensitization and reprocessing: A new discovery. *Journal of Near-Death Studies, 18*(3), 181–209.

Botkin, A. L., & Hannah, M. T. (2013). Brief report: Psychotherapeutic outcomes reported by therapists trained in Induced After-Death Communication. *Journal of Near-Death Studies, 31*(4), 221–224.

Botkin, A. L., with Hogan, R. C. (2005). *Induced after-death communication: A new therapy for healing grief and trauma.* Charlottesville, VA: Hampton Roads.

Foster, R. D., James, D., & Holden, J. M. (2009). Practical applications of near-death experiences research. In J. M. Holden, B. Greyson, & D. James (Eds.), *The handbook of near-death experiences: Thirty years of investigation* (pp. 235–258). Santa Barbara, CA: Praeger/ABC-CLIO.

Guggenheim, B., & Guggenheim, J. (1996). *Hello from heaven!* New York, NY: Bantam Doubleday Dell.

Hannah, M. T., Botkin, A. L., Marrone, J. G., & Streit-Horn, J. (2013). Brief report: Induced After-Death Communication: An update. *Journal of Near-Death Studies, 31*(4), 213–220.

Holden, J. M. (2012). Hourglass of love. In J. Canfield, M. V. Hansen, & A. Newmark (Eds.), *Chicken soup for the soul: Messages from heaven* (pp. 55–57). Cos Cob, CT: Chicken Soup for the Soul.

Knight, M. T. (2011). *Ways of being: The alchemy of bereavement and communiqué* (Unpublished doctoral thesis). University of Sydney, Sydney, Australia.

Streit-Horn, J. (2011a). *A systematic review of research on after-death communication* (Doctoral dissertation). Retrieved from http://digital.library.unt.edu/ark:/67531/metadc84284/m1/

Ásatrú in Counseling

Cliff Hamrick

According to the United States Census Bureau, as of 2011, there were just under 700,000 self-identified Wiccans and Neo-Pagans living in the US. The number of self-identified members of New Religious Movements—including Wicca, Pagan, and Druid—doubled from the years 2000 to 2008 (Kosmin & Keysar, 2008). This number is most likely an underestimation due to the number of Wiccans and Neo-Pagans who are not open about their beliefs (Ezzy & Berger, 2009). Spirituality and religion can be positive resources for clients to improve well-being and client outcomes in therapy (Worthington, Hook, Davis, & McDaniel, 2011).

Ásatrú is a religion of Neo-Paganism with origins in Northern Europe that is gaining increasing interest around the world. The term "Ásatrú" is taken from two Icelandic words (*Aesir* and *tru*) and roughly translates as "true to the Aesir." The Aesir were some of the deities worshipped historically by Norse and Germanic peoples; these deities include Odin, Thor, and Frigga. Though the official formation of this religion dates to the early 1970s in Iceland, the roots of the religion reach back to Pagan Europe and prehistory. A common reason that most Ásatrúar (the term for adherents) follow Ásatrú is their desire to reclaim an ancestry that was lost during the Christianization of Northern Europe. That said, there are also Ásatrúar of varying ethnicities (Paxson, 2006, p. 156).

The purpose of this chapter is to introduce counselors to the beliefs and practices of Ásatrú and to discuss how those beliefs and practices can be useful to clients, regardless of the clients' spiritual beliefs.

Common Beliefs of Ásatrú

One of the difficulties of explaining the beliefs of a Pagan religion to non-pagans is that there is no single reference to provide guidance or dogma. So, when discussing the beliefs of any Pagan religion, it is important to note that individuality within the Pagan community means that there is no common set of beliefs that are held by all of its members, and it is important to discuss with the client the intricacies of their own belief systems rather than make assumptions.

Like all other Pagan religions, Ásatrú is polytheistic, with male and female deities. Odin, the leader of the gods, is known for his one eye, which he sacrificed to gain the wisdom to use the runes properly (Hollander, 1962, p. 5). He won the knowledge of the runes by hanging himself from the World Tree for nine days and nights. Thor, the god of lightning and thunder, is the most popular of gods thanks, in part, to Marvel comics. He is known for his many battles with frost giants and is seen as a protector of humanity from the chaos of nature. Frey, one of the gods from Vanaheim, one of the realms of the gods, was considered the god of kings in Sweden; before the rise of Christianity there the royal family traced their lineage back to him. His sister, Freya, is a goddess from Vanaheim. She is associated with fertility, beauty, and sexuality. She brought the Germanic form of shamanism, *seidr*, with her and taught it to Odin and humanity. Some scholars believe that she provides the original concept of witches today. Other gods and goddesses found in Ásatrú include Frigga, Odin's wife; Loki, the trickster god; Njord, the father of Frey and Freya and the god of the sea; and Tyr, who sacrificed his sword hand to help the gods contain the monstrous Fenris.

An interesting concept in Ásatrú is that, according to mythology, the gods will die and the world will be destroyed in Ragnarok, a great battle against the children of Loki (Jennings, 2003, p. 26). The myths even describe who will kill whom and how each will die. Because the gods know this battle is coming, Odin gathers up slain warriors to stay with him in his hall, Valhalla. Many Ásatrúar believe that if they live a good life and they fight well for worthy causes, when they die they will also go to Valhalla. Those who are deemed unworthy go to Helheim, which, rather than being a place of punishment, is simply a boring existence.

Ancestry and community are important in Ásatrú. Many Ásatrúar study their family trees and trace their lineages back as far as possible. For many Ásatrúar, following their faith is also a way of reconnecting with an ancient past that they believe was stolen from them, much in the same way that Native Americans believe that their culture and language was taken from them (Smith, 2007).

Like other Pagan religions, Ásatrú uses a form of magic. Runes are the primary form of magical workings in Ásatrú. Most people associate the runes with divination, but runes are also used for defensive and offensive magical workings. Each rune is associated with a different concept. For instance, *fehu* is associated with wealth, and *uruz* is associated with strength. Those who study the runes find many layers of understanding and connection. Many people, even those who do not practice Ásatrú, use the runes for divination. But, by combining different runes, one can create a "bind rune" that has a specific magical effect, based upon the runes used and their associations. Historically, these were used to heal, protect, and even curse.

Within Ásatrú, there are two important rituals: *blót* and *sumble*. The blót, pronounced 'bloat,' refers to a feast and/or sacrifice at which the Ásatrúar offer gifts and praise to the gods. The sumble is a ritual in which a drinking horn filled with beer or mead is passed around a group of Ásatrúar. The beer or mead is drunk to remember those who are worthy of a special honor, to offer a prayer or oath, or to boast of a personal accomplishment. The sumble is a tradition still practiced today in the form of a eulogy at a funeral or a toast at a wedding.

Seidr, pronounced 'seethe,' fills the role of Germanic shamanism within Ásatrú. Like most other shamanistic practices, seidr uses drumming and chanting to induce a trance state. During this trance, the practitioner may go on spirit journeys or try to divine the future. Almost nothing was written down concerning the actual practices of seidr. Consequently, modern practitioners must rediscover their knowledge from sages and extant data on shamanistic cultures found in Northern Europe. As a part of seidr, the *alfar*—nature spirits of the land, sea, and sky—were revered.

Honor, values, and character are very important to Ásatrúar. One of the texts that has survived from the thirteenth century is the *Hávamál* (Bray & Ashliman, 2003), which translates as *Sayings of the High One*; the High One is generally considered to be Odin. The Hávamál is a long poem with hundreds of stanzas that appears to have four parts. The first part, referred to as the "Guest's Section," reads much like a list of common sense sayings along the lines of "you can lead a horse to water, but you can't make him drink" or "never look a gift horse in the mouth." The second section tells the tale of Odin seducing a giant's daughter to steal the Mead of Poetry. The third section is similar to the "Guest Section" in that Odin is instructing a dwarf, Loddfáfnir, on how to be a good person, reiterating much of the wisdom found in the Guest Section. The last part of the Hávamál is the "Rune Song" in which Odin tells the tale of how he learned the runes and the power they hold.

Focusing on the "Guest's Section" and the instructions to the dwarf, some Ásatrúar have found themes that seem to recur. These Ásatrúar have come up with a list called the Nine Noble Virtues, which are Courage, Truth, Honor, Fidelity, Discipline, Hospitality, Industriousness, Self-reliance, and Perseverance. Ásatrúar use this list as well as the teachings in the Hávamál as a guide to how to live a proper life, which will lead to an afterlife in Valhalla.

Ásatrú Concepts in Counseling

When working with Ásatrúar or non-Ásatrúar clients, some concepts within Ásatrú can be helpful with some clients and some issues. Any therapist using a strengths-based approach, such as solution-focused therapy or positive psychology, can find correlations within Ásatrú. In some ways, Ásatrú is not a religion of beliefs but a religion of values. Within the Hávamál and the Nine Noble Virtues are values and strengths to which a client can aspire. When working with some Pagan clients, I refer to the Hávamál to give examples of how they can gain inspiration about how to deal with the problems they face. For instance, stanza 71 in the Hávamál (Bray & Ashliman, 2003) reads:

The lame man can ride a horse,
the handless man is a herdsman,
The deaf be a strong fighter,
To be blind is better than to burn on a pyre:
There is nothing a corpse can do.

This stanza conveys that no matter how bad a person's situation may be, it is still preferable to being dead. This stanza can be helpful when working with clients suffering from depression and suicidal ideation by pointing out that everyone, regardless of their abilities or current situation, can still do something constructive with their lives. Everyone has a purpose, and everyone can serve others. However, to be dead is pointless because there is nothing that corpses can do. In stanza 12, the Hávamál (Bray & Ashliman, 2003) also addresses the problem of alcoholism:

Less good than one would believe
Is mead for the sons of men:
A man knows less the more he drinks,
And becomes a befuddled fool.

I found this stanza rather surprising, considering the stereotypical image of a Viking as a dirty, ale-guzzling barbarian. However, the same culture that gave the world Viking raiders also admonished against too much alcohol. I use this stanza with clients dealing with substance abuse, particularly alcoholism. I use it to demonstrate that too much alcohol has been a problem for centuries and is nothing new. Also, this stanza helps put the issue in context that many people suffer from this problem, and they are not alone.

Runes can also be used in therapy. A rune is a simple image that can carry a deep meaning. Though I do not use runes as a divinatory tool in counseling, I will recommend a rune to a client as a reminder of a useful or positive concept. For instance, the rune uruz symbolizes the strength and tenacity of the aurochs, an extinct species of wild cattle. Clients who are feeling weak and powerless can carry a representation of this rune with them and then look at it to remind them of the strength that they do have. Fehu symbolizes wealth and can be carried to remind clients who have the problem of worrying about the future to remember a sense of abundance in their lives. Runes work well because they are simple line drawings, and many appear to be just letters from the alphabet; for example, *gebo* is an 'x,' and *wunjo* is a 'p.' The simplicity of runes provides clients with an opportunity to carry a rune clandestinely if they do not wish to make this method of support known to others. Also, because the runes are simple to draw, clients can write them on a piece of paper or even draw the rune over their foreheads or hearts to bring the symbology within them.

The rituals of blót and sumble can be of use to certain clients. Blót is at its heart a ritual of gratitude. When Ásatrúars perform a blót, they are essentially thanking the gods, the spirits, and their ancestors for what they have in their lives and giving up a bit of their success to celebrate it. Taking this essence, clients dealing with anxiety and/or depression can be offered the homework to spend time each day being thankful for what they have. Based on my clinical experience, I have found that often clients focus too much attention on what they lack, and this focus leads them to forget how much they really have going for them. This is a common concept within positive psychology to help clients focus on their strengths and resources rather than their weaknesses and deficits. With clients who feel that they truly have nothing to be thankful for, I interject suggestions like being thankful for their health, their security, their ability to come to therapy, and the like. An aspect of a sumble is the boast. Though there are admonishments against boasting in the Hávamál (Bray & Ashliman, 2003), it seems that it was acceptable to be boastful during a sumble. This concept is useful with clients dealing with low self-esteem. Getting clients to say out loud to the therapist or even to themselves that they are competent and worthy of respect can greatly boost their self-esteem. Again, with these clients there may need to be some coaching, but I have never found a person who isn't good at something.

Shamanism has had a role in therapy since Carl Jung introduced the ideas of archetypes (Jung & Franz, 1964). Within Ásatrú, the use of seidr allows clients to tap into a deeper spiritual resource, which can have benefits in therapy. For some clients, this practice may take the form of a shamanic journey or guided meditation in the therapist's office. For other clients, they may feel more at home with dream analysis with the therapist's guidance. Other clients may simply have a totem animal or mythological figure with which they identify strongly. Any of these tools can be used to gain insight into the problems facing clients and possible solutions to resolve them. The relationships with these symbols and archetypes are very personal and must be taken on a case-by-case basis with each client. It is even possible that, for a particular client, the meaning of each of these symbols may change over time, and it is important to check in with the client to gauge any changes from the past.

Conclusion

To date, research has not been published addressing the use of Ásatrú in counseling. Thus, it fits the American Counseling Association's ethical designation as a "developing or innovative [technique/procedure/ modality]" (American Counseling Association, 2014, p. 10, standard C.7.a.), which requires counselors to exercise relevant ethical practice such as informing clients of that designation.

With that stipulation in mind, for Ásatrúar, utilizing the concepts listed above can greatly facilitate therapy. Even if the therapist is not fully versed in Ásatrú lore or mythology, showing an interest in and appreciation for an Ásatrúar client's beliefs may quickly build rapport and have a positive impact on client outcomes. Ásatrú draws upon a long and rich history and a culture that still holds fascination today. Though Ásatrú is specific to a particular culture, this culture is can be seen in the present. Some of humanity's rituals (sumble), holidays (Christmas and Easter), and even the days of the week ('Thor's Day' and 'Frey's Day') have carried on from the time of the Vikings to modern society. This persistence indicates that more of this culture is accessible to clients than might immediately seem evident.

Suggested Resources

Print

Gerrard, K. (2011). *Seidr: The gate is open.* London, UK: Avalonia.

Jennings, P. (2003). *The northern tradition* (2nd ed.). Somerset, UK: Capall Bann.

Jennings, P. (2007). *Heathen paths: Viking and Anglo Saxon Pagan beliefs.* Somerset, UK: Capall Bann.

Lindow, J. (2001). *Norse mythology: A guide to the gods, heroes, rituals, and beliefs.* Santa Barbara, CA: Oxford University Press.

Paxson, D. L. (2005). *Taking up the runes: A complete guide to using runes in spells, rituals, divination, and magic.* San Francisco, CA: Weiser Books.

Paxson, D. L. (2006). *Essential Ásatrú: Walking the path of Norse Paganism.* New York, NY: Kensington.

References

American Counseling Association. (2014). *Code of ethics.* Alexandria, VA: Author.

Bray, O. (Trans.) & Ashliman, D. L. (Ed.). (2003). *Hávamál: The words of Odin the high one.* Retrieved from http://pitt.edu/~dash/havamal.html

Ezzy, D., & Berger, H. (2009). Witchcraft: Changing patterns of participation in the early twenty-first century. *Pomegranate, 11,* 165–180.

Hollander, L. (1962). *The poetic Edda.* Austin, TX: University of Texas Press.

Jung, C. G., & Franz, M. (1964). *Man and his symbols.* New York, NY: Picador.

Kosmin, B. A., & Keysar, A. (2008). *American Religious Identification Survey (ARIS).* Retrieved from http://commons.trincoll.edu/aris/files/2011/08/ARIS_Report_2008.pdf

Smith, A. (2007). *Soul wound: The legacy of Native American schools.*
      Retrieved from http://www.amnestyusa.org/node/87342
United States Census Bureau. (2011). *Statistical abstract of the United States
      2011.* Retrieved from http://www.census.gov/compendia/statab/2012/
      tables/12s0075.pdf
Worthington, E. L. Jr., Hook, J. N., Davis, D. E., & McDaniel, M. (2011).
      Religion and spirituality. *Journal of Clinical Psychology: In Session, 67*(2),
      204–214.

Creative Visualization

TRANSFORMING ONE'S WORLD THROUGH IMAGERY

Carol A. Fournier

Creative visualization is the concentrated engagement of imagination to affect change in integrative therapeutic care designed to support the wellbeing of the mind, body, heart, and spirit. There are two contexts for engaging this classic intervention of active imagination. The first is personally directed, and the second is guided by another person whereby the one being guided listens to the images being shared and uses one's own imagination to engage the story.

Creative visualization, also known as mental imagery, guided imagery, or active imagination, is a therapeutic intervention applied in psychotherapy, healthcare, education, athletic, and religious or spiritual practice, with general as well as specific outcomes and goals. Psychologist Jean Kristeller (2011), in "Spirituality and Meditation," observed that "generally, the initial goal of guided meditative practice is to cultivate awareness around the targeted issue, evoke associations . . . and to increase the capacity to suspend or modify the usual cognitive, behavioral, or emotional reactions to these experiences" (p. 205).

The use of imagery engages the conscious and the unconscious aspects of the mind including the symbolism, signs, and meaning-making associations that unfold in communal and individual internalized memory. Human minds store complex pieces of information through image. Memories store emotionally and behaviorally charged triggers that can have both creative and repressive qualities. People's narratives are often stored in the form of image. Imagery contains meaning and influences thoughts, words, actions, feelings, behavior, and outcomes.

Creative visualization is different from relaxation exercises or biofeedback techniques. Relaxation exercises are primarily focused on releasing stress both physically and psychologically. Biofeedback is a technique of increasing awareness and management of biological functions such as breath, heart rate, and respiration. By contrast, creative visualization is designed to create change by stimulating the active imagination of the cognitive and neural functioning of the brain.

History

If measured from the estimated founding of Hinduism (2000 BCE) and Judaism (1500 BCE), creative visualization as a therapeutic technique has been utilized in spiritual and religious sociocultural contexts for over 4,000 years. The use of imagery as a healing practice in indigenous Native communities, such as the Native American, First Nation (Canadian), and aboriginal African, Asian, and European cultures, may predate this estimate. Prior to the founding of Western psychology, the stewards of the contemplative and creative practices of these religious paths were the primary "doctors" of "divine therapy" utilizing proven methods to maximize wellbeing of mind, heart, body, and spirit in relationship with self, community, and the Mystery of creation (Keating, 1997; Newburg & Waldman, 2009; O'Kane, 1981; Pargament, 1997; Smith, 1991; Verman & Shapiro, 1996). The contemporary language of creative visualization or the practice of guided or mental imagery has emerged as the counseling and healthcare fields attempt to define, measure, and quantify the most efficacious usage of ancient spiritual and religious practices.

Carl Gustav Jung, the founder of Analytic Psychology, strongly influenced psychotherapy by engaging the study and therapeutic use of images, dreams, art, and active imagination to support positive outcomes in psychological and spiritual wellbeing. In 1903, Jung's dissertation initiated a lifelong scientific exploration of the psyche and the role and influence of the imagination on the human experience. (Jung, 1934/1996). During the 1970s, contributors to the study of creative visualization in the psychotherapeutic and healthcare fields included Herbert Benson, Irving Oyle, Carl and Stephanie Simonton, Roberto Assagioli, David Bresler, and Martin Rossman.

Imagery, Imagination, and Cognitive Process

Our minds are constructed to be constantly scanning both our external and internal environments for danger and for sources of pleasure. The mind is also always interpreting, preparing for action, and solving problems, and such processing may be dominant over our abilities to become quiet, to listen to a higher level of inner self, to engage wisdom. (Kristeller 2011, p. 208)

A foundation for the use of imagery in counseling and psychotherapy begins with an understanding of the nature and process of imagery. Whereas thoughts are verbal, images are sensory. For example, images can be visual (imagine the appearance of a room with which you are familiar), auditory (imagine the sound of wind chimes), tactile (imagine a benevolent, caring touch), olfactory (imagine the smell of a flower), or kinesthetic (imagine the feeling of keeping your balance). The presentation of images and their associated meanings are unique to each person. Images have personal, communal, anthropological, and global meanings that people interpret through both conscious and unconscious processes informed by their socio-cultural contexts. In the process of creative visualization, intrinsic and extrinsic knowledge combine with unconscious processes, offering new information, insight, and options that may previously have been repressed or as-yet undiscovered (Jung, 1962; Keating, 1997; Rossman, 2000; Singer, 2005).

Two Imagery Processes

As there are a number of methods of concentration and contemplation (meditation) that serve to accomplish the goals of creative visualization, two approaches are included here as a foundation. The first approach is designed to help the visualizer to change thought and behavior patterns by imagining new possibilities. The process involves four steps:

1. Clearing and emptying the mind and heart to create a space for new possibilities to emerge. This step can be achieved through a variety of activities such as focusing on the breath, stillness, or an external object; being aware of thoughts; or selecting a word that can maintain focus and using the word in a repetitive fashion.
2. Consciously creating or reflecting on an image, feeling, concept, thought, or experience and imagining possibilities that might happen within the scene. It is important that the details of the

creative visualization first begin in a broad manner and then become more realistic and specific.

3. Affirming the inspiration or insight that comes through the practice so that it becomes rooted in the individual's mind, body, and emotions.

4. Returning to the practice again over time to reaffirm the desired outcome from the practice—or, alternately, returning to the practice in the broadest form and consciously paying attention to the new possibilities and perspectives that emerge. In either case, new learning informs the affirmations that are unfolding to support transformation and wellbeing. (Fournier, 2012–2014)

The second approach is for use in spiritually or religiously oriented counseling. It involves five steps:

1. Same as step 1 above. For some individuals, the process can be facilitated by the connection with an image of nature, such as a garden or the visual or auditory connection with an icon, symbol, or image that relates to their personal spiritual or faith path.

2. Creating or imagining a scene that represents some aspect of one's Divine Ideal or Ultimate Reality.

3. Envisioning oneself within the context of the scene and in relationship to the Ideal.

4. Contemplating various aspects of this Ideal and how they relate to one's spiritual journey.

5. Affirming the insights and inspiration that may come through the practice so it can become rooted in the person's experience of wellbeing and purpose. (O'Kane, 1981)

Evidence-Based Outcomes

Clinical trials and qualitative research since the 1970s have contributed to an understanding of imagery as it applies to a variety of presenting psychological and biological concerns. Scientists and healthcare professionals have demonstrated its positive effect and contributions to evidence-based practice (Benson, 1975; Collins & Rice, 1997; Cupal & Brewer, 2001; Dusek et al., 2008; Graffa & Johnson, 1987; Hornyak & Green, 2000; Klaus, Beniaminovitz, Choi, Greenfield, Whitworth,

Oz, & Mancini, 2000; Koenig, 2008; Koenig, King, & Carson, 2012; Kristeller, 2011; Newhan & Balamuth, 1990–1991; Rockefeller, Serlin, & Fox, 2007; Singer, 2005; Tusek, Church, & Fazio, 1997; Tusek, Cwynar, & Cosgrove, 1999; Weil & Rossman, n.d.)

In recent decades, clinical understanding of the importance of image, imagination, and creativity in psychotherapy has expanded substantially. A selective analysis of guided imagery (creative visualization) research conducted between 1984 and 2007 provided substantial evidence of its efficacy for increasing feelings of wellbeing, reducing depression and anxiety, reducing pain and the need for pain medication, changing behavior related to chronic health conditions, and increasing comfort and alleviating symptoms associated with a variety of types of psychological and physiological pain (Rockefeller et al., 2007). In studies funded through the U.S. Department of Veteran Affairs, such as the Durham Study begun in 2007, researchers have attempted to measure the efficacy of creative imagery (guided imagery) for recovery from trauma combined with MRIs and blood testing as well as PTSD clinical assessment (United States Department of Veteran Affairs, 2007).

Creative visualization has been used to improve academic and athletic performance, enhance wellbeing through lifestyle changes, manage chronic pain and psychological stressors, and treat and manage symptoms of cancer, heart disease, and other health conditions. Creative visualization can assist in alleviating depression, anxiety, and symptoms associated with PTSD and autism; with rehabilitation from injury that resulted in limited mobility or the need to retrain musculature; in post-surgical recovery; and in the cultivation of overall satisfaction through an increase in awareness of life purpose and a completion of life goals (Achterberg, Dossey, & Kolkmeier, 1994; Cobb, Puchalshi, & Rumbold, 2012; Koenig, 2008; Rockefeller et al., 2007).

Cautions and Contraindications Informed by Multicultural Sensitivities

Spiritually oriented counseling engages creative visualization and imagery through a sociocultural spiritual and religious world context as adapted to the psychotherapeutic process. The adaptation of traditional spiritual and religious practices receives a mixed response from some religious communities. In regards to creative visualization, some people find that the use of mind-altering modalities does not align with their essential faith, theology, or religious practice. Some individuals believe that such practices place the individual self at the center of the story and do not provide spaciousness for the existence and influence of a Creative Mystery or God that influences the individual outside of one's own personal experience. When recommending the therapeutic usage of creative visualization or guided imagery, it is important to assess the individual's spiritual and religious culture to determine the extent to which creative visualization is compatible with one's beliefs.

The use of creative visualization might be contraindicated in cases where individuals have limited creative capacity to visualize. The use of a photography, painting, or spiritual or religious icon could assist with supporting the cultivation of active imagination. The use of art therapy interventions, such as creating mandalas or montages, that can give form to an expression of creativity may assist in laying the foundation for use of creative visualization through a progressive treatment strategy.

For individuals who present with symptoms of delusions or hallucinations, the use of creative visualization may be contraindicated. However, Jung documented clinical success when working with active imagination and art to clarify and create a didactic relationship with material that could be further integrated by clients with a variety of delusional or psychotic features (Jung, 1962, 1996). Further research in these areas is warranted.

Not all images are created equal in value to elicit positive outcomes in a therapeutic context. Some use of creative visualization can have a negative effect on wellbeing. For example, a counselor might inadvertently draw on an image to which a client has a traumatic or other symptom-activating association, such as a train station for a client whose family was forcibly deported by train, or an elevator for a client with claustrophobia or panic attacks. Therefore, counselors using creative visualization do best to first take a thorough client history; in this way, sensitivity to symbols, signs, images, color, and light can assist in mitigating the negative associations or creating more affirming mental imagery processes as therapeutically indicated. The counselor who inadvertently activates client distress can use any of a number of strategies to reduce distress, including relaxation and image substitution.

Conclusion

Counselors can enhance their practice through the professional use of creative visualization by receiving training in the process and usage of the technique, as it can be applied across a variety of psychotherapeutic treatment areas. Considering that the process of engaging the imagination can create change, understanding clients' presenting conditions and worldviews combined with assessment of their meaning-making symbolism, spirituality, and religious beliefs can enhance effectiveness. Although creative visualization can be easily learned, continuing education in its implementation with a variety of presenting conditions is essential for positive, focused outcomes. Integrative care, particularly when chronic health conditions co-present with psychological healing processes, can enhance outcomes while building successful collaborative care teams (Cobb et al., 2012; Koenig, 2008).

In conclusion, creative visualization is an essential sensory, cognitive, emotive, and holistic process of integrating the conscious and unconscious aspects of the mind to transform patterns and outcomes. Creative visualization can enhance overall wellbeing, decrease distractibility, and increase a sense of self-control and actualization while assisting with the management of complex bio-psycho-social-spiritual concerns. Research specific to presenting psychological, spiritual, and religious concerns could further understanding about technique as well as short- and long-term efficacy in supporting wellbeing and enhancing individual purpose and meaning making outcomes in life. The spiritual and religious wisdom of the ages is confirmed in the quantitative and qualitative inquiry into the profound flexibility and efficacy of creative visualization in manifesting positive change restoring wellbeing of body, mind, heart, and spirit.

Suggested Resources

Online

Journal of Mental Imagery (JMI): http://www.journalofmentalimagery .com/ This groundbreaking journal, dedicated solely to the study of mental imagery, has served as the major forum for original and creative thought on mental imagery since it was established in 1977. It offers timely, peer-reviewed articles, theme issues, and open peer commentary. Committed to scholarship, dialogue, and debate on mental imagery,

JMI has received critical acclaim around the world from researchers, theoreticians, clinicians, and educators. It is a vital and invaluable resource for individuals and libraries interested in research, theory, and applications in this rapidly growing field.

References

Achterberg, J., Dossey, B., & Kolkmeier, L. (1994). *Rituals of healing: Using imagery for health and wellness.* New York, NY: Bantam Books.
Benson, H. (1975). *The relaxation response.* New York, NY: William Morrow.
Cobb, M., Puchalski, C., & Rumbold, B. (Eds). (2012). *Spirituality in healthcare.* Oxford, UK: Oxford University Press.
Collins, J. A., & Rice, V. H. (1997). Effects of relaxation intervention in phase II cardiac rehabilitation: Replication and extension. *Heart & Lung, 26*(1), 31–44.
Cupal, D. D., & Brewer, B. W. (2001). Effects of relaxation and guided imagery on knee strength, reinjury anxiety and pain following anterior cruciate ligament reconstruction. *Rehabilitative Psychology, 46*(1), 28–43.
Dusek, J. A., Hibberd, P. L., Buczynski, B., Chang, B. H., Dusek, K. C., Johnston, J. M., . . . Zusman, R. M. (2008). Stress management versus lifestyle modification on systolic hypertension and medication elimination: A randomized trial. *Journal of Alternative and Complementary Medicine, 14*, 129–138. doi:10.1089/acm.207.0623.
Fournier, C. A. (2012–2014). Guided imagery for health. Unpublished raw data.
Graffa, S., & Johnson, A. (1987). A comparison of two relaxation strategies for the relief of pain and its distress. *Journal of Pain & Symptom Management, 2*, 229–231.
Hornyak, L., & Green, J. (2000). *Healing from within: The use of hypnosis in women's health care.* Washington, DC: American Psychological Association.
Jung, C. G., (1996). *The archetypes and the collective unconscious.* Princeton, NJ: Princeton University Press (Original work published 1934).
Jung, C. G. (1962). *Memories, dreams, reflections.* New York, NY: Vintage Books.
Keating, T. (1997). *Active meditations for contemplative prayer.* New York, NY: Continuum.
Klaus, L., Beniaminovitz, A., Choi, L, Greenfield, F., Whitworth, G. C., Oz, M. C., & Mancini, D. M. (2000). Pilot study of guided imagery use in

patients with severe heart failure. *American Journal of Cardiology, 86,* 101–104.

Koenig, H. G. (2008). *Medicine, religion & health: Where science and spirituality meet.* West Conshohocken, PA: Templeton Foundation Press.

Koenig, H. G., King, D. E, & Carson, V. B. (2012). *Handbook of religion and health.* Oxford, UK: Oxford University Press.

Kristeller, J. (2011). Spirituality and meditation. In J. D. Aten, M. R. McMinn, & E. L. Worthington Jr. (Eds.), *Spiritually oriented interventions for counseling and psychotherapy* (pp. 197–227). Washington, DC: American Psychological Association.

Newberg, A. B., & Waldman, M. (2009). *How God changes your brain.* New York, NY: Ballantine Books.

Newhan, G., & Balamuth, R. (1990–1991). Use of imagery in chronic pain outpatient group. *Imagination, Cognition & Personality, 10*(1), 25–38.

O'Kane, A. (1981). *Making your ideal a reality: A study of the counseling approach developed by Pir Vilayat Inayat Khan* (Unpublished master's thesis). Goddard College, Plainfield, VT.

Pargament, K. (1997). *The psychology of religion and coping: Theory, research, practice.* New York, NY: Guilford Press.

Rockefeller, K., Serlin, I. A., & Fox, J. (2007). Multimodal imagery and healthcare. In I. A. Serlin, K. Rockefeller, & S. Brown (Eds.), *Whole person healthcare, Vol. 2: Psychology, spirituality & health* (pp. 63–81). Westport, CT: Praeger.

Rossman, M. L. (2000). *Guided imagery for self-healing: An essential resource for anyone seeking wellness.* Tiburon, CA: H. J. Kramer Books.

Serlin, I. A., Rockefeller, K., & Brown, S. (Eds). (2007). *Whole person healthcare, Vol. 2: Psychology, spirituality, and healthcare.* Westport, CT: Praeger.

Singer, J. L. (2005). *Imagery in psychotherapy.* Washington, DC: American Psychological Association.

Smith, H. (1991). *The world's religions.* San Francisco, CA: HarperSanFrancisco.

Tusek, D., Church, J. M., & Fazio, V. W. (1997). Guided imagery as a coping strategy for perioperative patients. *AORN Journal, 66,* 644–649.

Tusek, D. L., Cwynar, R., & Cosgrove, D. M. (1999). Effect of guided imagery on length of stay, pain, and anxiety in cardiac surgery. *Journal of Cardiovascular Management, 10*(2), 22–28.

United States Department of Veterans Affairs. (2007). *Durham study to probe benefits of guided imagery for PTSD* [PDF document]. Retrieved

from http://www.research.va.gov/resources/pubs/docs/va_research
_currents_july_07.pdf

Verman, M., & Shapiro, D. H. (1996). Jewish meditation: Context and content, historical background, types, and purpose. In Y. Haruki, Y. Ishii, & M. Suzuki. (Eds.), *Comparative and psychological study of meditation* (pp. 95–120). Delft, Netherlands: Eburon.

Weil, A., & Rossman, M. (n.d.). *Self-healing with guided imagery: How to use your mind to heal your body* [abridged audiobook]. Louisville, CO: Sounds True.

Deathbed Phenomena, Quantum Physics, and the Survival of Consciousness

Linda L. Smith
Peggy Lesniewicz

In the last quarter of the twentieth century, a new generation of scientists began researching topics previously considered to belong only within the realm of religion or parapsychology. Many of these topics involved the experience of death, and one of the most provocative was the survival of consciousness beyond the biological death of the body. Psychiatrist Raymond Moody must be given much of the credit for convincing scientists and laypeople alike that such concepts are fit subjects for scientific research—which was certainly not an easy task. However, his 1975 classic book, *Life After Life*, presented persuasive evidence of a distinct phenomenon, the now widely known near-death experience (NDE), with a quantifiable set of common elements that appeared across a number of cultures, religions, and nationalities. His case studies demonstrated that many individuals, when near death or actually clinically dead, showed evidence of the capability of perception, cognition, and memory—even when it appeared impossible for them to have any level of brain activity or consciousness. Subsequent research on NDEs showed similar results reported by a wide range of individuals around the globe (Holden, 2009; Long, 2010; Osis & Haraldsson, 1977; Parnia, 2006; Ring, 1980; Scott, 1978; van Lommel, 2010; Wilson, 1987).

Moody was followed by a long series of scientists who further expanded the permissible boundaries of science into what was once considered the exclusive territory of religion. Now in the second decade of the twenty-first century, interest in such topics has become widespread.

Hardly a week goes by without a new book being released about someone dead or dying visiting what they often identify as heaven; and more and more frequently it is not a born-again Christian but a physician or a scientist who is relating the story (e.g., neurosurgeon Eben Alexander, 2012; orthopedist Mary Neal, 2012). In fact, many of the researchers into this new realm of science are themselves physicians who were drawn into the field after repeatedly hearing about such experiences from their patients. In addition to NDEs, many other topics are being investigated that touch on the existence of consciousness independent of the body or brain. In an out-of-body experience (OBE), frequently but not always associated with NDEs, the subject reports his or her consciousness leaving and floating above the body with full awareness and perception of its surroundings. Subjects often later report seeing and hearing events during the experience that they had no normal way of knowing (Holden, 2009; van Lommel, 2010). Similarly, after awakening from coma, some patients report experiences when they were unconscious, such as floating down the hospital hallway or even leaving the hospital altogether, and observing events or conversations they could not have perceived through normal sensory perception.

Deathbed visions (DBVs) and so-called deathbed coincidences (DBCs) represent a wide range of reports of experiences that appear to further substantiate the existence of consciousness separate from and independent of the physical body. Researchers have collected many of these reports by surveying hospice and nursing home workers about their experiences with dying patients and their families (Brayne, Lovelace, & Fenwick, 2008; Brayne, Farnham, & Fenwick, 2006; Fenwick, Lovelace, & Brayne, 2007, 2009). DBVs occur when an individual who is dying reports seeing individuals not visible to others in the room. These experiences are often labeled hallucinations or delusions, terms that are both disparaging and inaccurate if, in fact, the dying person is actually seeing something real that others, for whatever reason, cannot see. The individuals that appear in these reports are typically deceased loved ones, but in some cases they are strangers who seem benevolent in intent, angels or other religious figures, or even animals, including family pets (Fenwick & Brayne, 2011; Lerma, 2007; Muthumana, Kellehear, Kumar, & Moosa, 2010). It is not uncommon for dying individuals to report increasing numbers of "visitors" in the room as they grow nearer to death (Kessler, 2010). In rare cases, another person present in the room may also witness one of these visitors (Fenwick et al., 2009;

Fenwick & Brayne, 2011). Particularly interesting are cases when the apparition is a recently deceased person whose death was unknown to the individual nearing death (Greyson, 2010). In addition to seeing figures, the dying may also report seeing beautiful, light-filled, or heavenly landscapes. It is not uncommon at or near the moment of death for the one dying to look past the people surrounding the deathbed and toward the ceiling or a corner of the room, with an expression of awe and joy. The overwhelming majority of these experiences are perceived as comforting and reassuring, and those dying often feel the visitors have come to guide their transition into the next world (Houran, 1997; Kellehear, Pogonet, Mindruta-Stratan, & Gorelco, 2012).

A DBC, by contrast, is an event experienced by someone other than the dying individual. It is labeled "coincidence" because of the unusual juxtaposition of an event with or near the moment of a loved one's death—and often when the death of the loved one is not yet known. In some cases, a DBC can be a vision or dream by a close relative of the dead or dying loved one, often at a great geographical distance. Typically, such experiences occur approximately 30 minutes before or after the death, and shortly after the experience, the person who had the experience receives news of the death by phone or other means. Although any close family member or friend may appear to the living in such an experience, most frequently it is a first-degree relative, most commonly a grandmother appearing to a granddaughter (Fenwick et al., 2009; Fenwick & Brayne, 2011).

A second category of DBC does not involve a vision but rather some other unusual event that occurs at or near the moment of death. The most frequently reported examples are clocks and watches that stop precisely at the moment of the death. These may be in the room or house of the deceased or at the home of a relative, and the clock may be electric, battery-operated, or wind-up. It is also common for lights to flash, televisions to stop operating, or telephones to ring. There are even reports of entire phone conversations that were later found to have occurred after the death. Sometimes the family member feels a sense of the presence of the one who has just died, or smells cologne, cigar, or another fragrance associated with the deceased (Brayne et al., 2006; Fenwick et al., 2007; Fenwick, 2010; Guggenheim & Guggenheim, 1997).

Strong evidence for the survival of consciousness occurs during death-related phenomena when information is conveyed during death-related phenomena that is unknown to the receiver, the veracity of which can be later substantiated. Such instances are called veridical perception (Holden, 2009; van Lommel, 2010). Another group of verifiable perceptions is information purportedly received from deceased individuals through psychics or mediums. Although less frequently studied because of widespread disbelief in the possibility of such communication, some impressive research has been conducted, suggesting that remarkably specific, detailed, and accurate information might be received from such sources (Beischel, Boccuzzi, Biuso, & Rock, 2015; Schwartz, 2002).

Whether their afterlife beliefs include heaven, hell, nirvana, or universal consciousness, those with firm religious beliefs rarely question the survival of some kind of consciousness or soul in an afterlife. Nonbelievers, on the other hand, often feel obligated to deny the survival of consciousness based on their understanding of science. But is it good science to maintain the impossibility of consciousness existing without or beyond the body? As legitimate research into dying, death, and near-death phenomena increases, evidence mounts that information can be conveyed between humans across vast distances and perhaps even from beyond the grave. The concepts of quantum theory discussed below suggest the existence of a "non-local domain" beyond space and time that provides a possible explanation for the ability of the mind to exist independent of the brain. This research provides mental health professionals and spiritual directors a useful framework for examining unusual deathbed and near-death experiences from a scientific perspective that goes beyond the limitations of any traditional religious viewpoint. Examination of these concepts can validate believers' views about the survival of consciousness as well as help skeptics view these experiences in a broader, more accepting light. With this understanding, professionals are better able to help clients accept and integrate their experiences more successfully, whether they are believers, nonbelievers, or agnostics.

The Quantum World

No medical or physiological processes adequately explain the entire spectrum of death-related phenomena that have been documented, although many attempts have been made to do so (van Lommel, 2010). But the developing science of quantum physics presents a worldview that offers possible explanations for the apparent survival of conscious-ness beyond the body.

The quantum worldview runs counter to the paradigm of Western science and medicine, which explains why it is not widely understood or accepted, even though it had its origins in the first decade of the twen-tieth century. The currently prevailing Western paradigm is grounded in the philosophical concepts of materialism and reductionism. Mate-rialism holds that nothing exists other than matter and its complement, energy, and that nothing else is real. Reductionism maintains that all systems, no matter how complex, are merely the sum of their parts, and all their processes can be explained as results of those individual parts. Adherents to both materialism and reductionism deny the existence of anything that might be viewed as nonmaterial or supernatural, such as a soul, and they view the human mind or consciousness as exclusively caused by physical processes in the brain. These assumptions require the denial of the possibility of any type of consciousness separate from or independent of the brain. This view, widespread among American scientists and physicians, asserts that near-death and death-related phenomena are the product of delusions, hallucinations, medications, wishful thinking, the progress of disease, or other physical or chemical processes in the brain. Still in its infancy, quantum theory does not yet provide a comprehensive explanation of how consciousness might exist independent of the brain. However, it sufficiently undermines classical physics and the Western scientific paradigm to challenge the assump-tions on which denial of that possibility is based.

Reconstructing a worldview that more accurately reflects the real-ities shown by quantum theory begins with reconstructing a view of matter and its building block, the atom. The view of the atom, typi-cally portrayed as a tiny solar system with particles (electrons) spin-ning around a nucleus of other particles (protons and neutrons), is in many ways flawed. First, it is important to understand that the atom and all the matter made up of atoms, are almost entirely empty space. To understand just how much empty space is contained in an atom, it may be helpful to envision the population of the world. If all the empty space in the atoms of all the humans in the world were eliminated, the remaining particles would be about the size of a sugar cube (Chown, 2012). This example illustrates that the apparently solid matter that makes up humans' world, bodies, and brains is mostly emptiness. It merely appears solid and impenetrable because the electric charge of the atoms and molecules that make it up acts as a kind of magnet that prevents the matter of two objects from interpenetrating one another.

Second, the so-called particles that make up each atom are not really particles at all. The electrons, protons, and neutrons are, in turn, made up of other so-called elementary particles, which include quarks, leptons, and bosons (one of which is the recently discovered Higgs boson). These so-called particles are themselves, according to the current dominant view, M-theory, made up of something called "strings." These "strings" oscillate at varying frequencies to create the properties of the various particles they create. Whereas the universe exists in only four dimensions, the strings exist in 11 dimensions, somehow overlapping or contained inside the universe's four dimensions in a way that cannot readily be explained or envisioned. In reality, matter is not made up of particles at all, but rather is a kind of three-dimensional wave that creates a field that extends outward in all directions (Cole, 2001; McTaggart, 2002; Talbot, 2011).

Third, empty space is not really empty at all. As the above descriptions illustrate, rather than consisting of anything hard or solid, matter consists of an amorphous and fluid field, arising out of complex processes at the quantum level. These processes allow the continual creation of so-called virtual particles that pop into existence out of nothingness for the briefest of periods, and then pop back out of existence. The continual movement of these virtual particles is called quantum fluctuation or quantum vacuum fluctuation, and their interaction with other particles plays an important part in quantum processes (Moyer, 2012; Talbot, 2011).

Fourth, all matter in the universe is interconnected. According to this principle, called quantum entanglement, subatomic entities that were once united and then separated continue to influence one another, theoretically at great distances. Like all quantum principles, entanglement was postulated from mathematical calculations and later substantiated in a famous experiment by John Bell that was subsequently reproduced in many different contexts. He showed that when two protons are split apart, the properties of one can be changed at a distance by changing the properties of its twin (McEvoy & Zarate, 1997; Vedral, 2011). This effect is called non-locality, because it allows effects at a distance, apparently instantly and without traditional causation, in violation of classical physics theory. The concept of subatomic wormholes was developed to explain the apparent "communication" between particles.

Another interpretation uses the metaphor of a hologram to illustrate the interconnection of everything in the universe. A hologram is created by embedding on a special photographic-type plate an image that is produced in three-dimensional form when illuminated by laser light. When a hologram is broken into pieces, however, every fragment still contains and produces the entire three-dimensional image, albeit somewhat dimmer than the image from the whole. This metaphor is used to suggest that each fragment of the universe also contains all of the information contained in the whole (Talbot, 2011). Researchers are vigorously debating the role of information in the make-up of the universe, and one investigator has even devised an experiment to determine whether the foundation of space is digital (Moyer, 2012).

The principles of quantum theory briefly treated here result in a radically revised view of the foundational fabric of the universe, sometimes referred to as the non-local domain, quantum foam, or space-time foam. At the subatomic level, both the "nothingness" of space and the apparent solidity of matter are made up of continual fluctuations, similar to the appearance and disappearance of virtual particles described above. These fluctuations in the very fabric of space itself (more properly called "space-time," as the two are not separate) may create tiny "wormholes" that connect every point of space-time with every other point of space-time, thus allowing the effects of non-locality (McTaggart, 2002). In addition to suggesting how subatomic entities might "communicate," this concept of quantum foam suggests that all things, human minds included, arise out of the same source that at its base connects all of us humans to each other.

Quantum theory radically undermines the adequacy of traditional Newtonian physics, as well as the assumptions of materialism and reductionism, to explain all known phenomena. It should also supplant with finality the simplistic view that the mind and consciousness are caused only by the brain.

Researchers are only beginning to examine the result of quantum effects in complex biological systems, but support is already being found to show that it has effects there as well as at the subatomic level (Laszlo, 2008; Vedral, 2011). The causes and origins of human consciousness are still a mystery, and scientists continue to fiercely debate these topics (Koch, 2007). But there is no reason to believe that the matter making up the brain, which also arises out of the quantum foam, is not similarly affected by quantum effects such as entanglement and non-locality. Several prominent researchers of end-of-life phenomena have examined quantum theory as a way to explain some of the reported death-related experiences. Laszlo (2008), for example, cited the holographic field and non-locality concepts of quantum theory as possible explanations for communications allegedly received from the dead, arguing that consciousness is a holographic field carrying or having access to information in the non-local domain. Fenwick (2010) similarly used quantum theory to explain deathbed phenomena, suggesting that consciousness is an independent field rather than a product of the brain: "The hypothesis suggests that as death approaches, consciousness becomes loosened from the brain-mind structure, and this is the prime mover for the non-local effects that are noticed at this time" (p. 155). Perhaps Laszlo and Fenwick are on the right track, and one day scientists will discover that love between two people creates entanglement of their consciousness that binds and connects them at a distance—allowing communication even after death.

End-of-Life and Deathbed Considerations for Professional Caregivers

Examination of quantum theory provides mental health professionals and spiritual directors a useful framework for examining deathbed and near-death experiences from a scientific approach that goes beyond the limitations of a traditional religious viewpoint. We are not suggesting that professionals discuss quantum theory with their clients. Rather, we assert that an understanding of these concepts can provide a helpful background about the survival of consciousness. With this understanding, professionals are better able to help clients accept and integrate these experiences more successfully, whether they or their client are believers, nonbelievers, or agnostics.

With this understanding, caregivers can take several steps to help patients, clients, and their families understand, cope, and perhaps even transform their deathbed and other end-of-life experiences. The dying process is hard work that needs the support of concerned individuals. But before counselors can even start to help clients effectively, counselors need to examine their feelings and beliefs about their own and others' deaths, because these emotions and assumptions may cloud their ability to be helpful. Are counselors uncomfortable with the idea of their own death or fearful about the death of a loved one? Are counselors skeptical about end-of-life and deathbed phenomena that clients or their families may be experiencing? Are counselors convinced that survival of consciousness is impossible and that experiences suggesting otherwise are mere delusions? It is important that counselors are knowledgeable and open-minded about deathbed phenomena and how these can affect the dying and their families (Fenwick & Brayne, 2011; Fenwick et al., 2007). Without such open-mindedness, attempts at comforting clients may seem insincere or, even worse, cruel. It is important to remember that deathbed and other death-related experiences are almost always experienced as comforting, and counselors should be careful to do nothing that would deprive clients of such comfort during such a painful time (Fenwick et al., 2007).

Counselors should also be cognizant of the fears of the dying and be willing to talk with them about these fears (Groves, 2009). As always, what counselors bring to the dying client is themselves. It is important to provide a sense of connection and to be truly present to clients and listen to what is important to them. As a way of alleviating spiritual pain, the counselor should help clients resolve their unfinished business with their lives and relationships (Groves, 2009). In addition, if clients are experiencing deathbed visions or dreams about seeing deceased loved ones or the afterlife, it is important that they be allowed to talk about these experiences and that they be normalized and validated. It is also important to educate the family about such experiences to help them accept them as normal so they can support their loved one having these experiences (Mazzarino-Willett, 2010). For those experiencing post-death communication and deathbed coincidences, once again education and normalizing the experience is important (Fenwick et al., 2007). A judgment-free question that we have found effective is, "Was this experience comforting to you?" In all of the phenomena mentioned above, this is a good question to use, as it allows the client and family to begin talking freely about their experiences without fear of judgment.

Suggested Resources

Print

Brayne, S., Lovelace, H., & Fenwick, P. (2008). End-of-life experiences and the dying process in a Gloucestershire nursing home as reported by nurses and care assistants. *American Journal of Hospice & Palliative Medicine, 25*(3), 195–206.

Cole, K. (2001). *The hole in the universe: How scientists peered over the edge of emptiness and found everything.* San Diego, CA: Harcourt Books.

Fenwick, P., & Brayne, S. (2011). End-of-life experiences: Reaching out for compassion, communication, and connection—Meaning of deathbed visions and coincidences. *American Journal of Hospice & Palliative Medicine, 28*(1), 7–15.

Fenwick, P., Lovelace, H., & Brayne, S. (2009). Comfort for the dying: Five year retrospective and one year prospective studies of end of life experiences. *Archive of Gerontology and Geriatrics, 51*, 173–179.

Greyson, B. (2009). Near-death experiences and deathbed visions. In A. Kellehear (Ed.), *The study of dying* (pp. 253–275). New York, NY: Cambridge University Press.

Kessler, D. (2010). *Visions, trips, and crowded rooms: Who and what you see before you die.* Carlsbad, CA: Hay House.

Lerma, J. (2007). *Into the light: Real life stories about angelic visits, visions of the afterlife, and other pre-death experiences.* Franklin Lakes, NJ: New Page Books.

McTaggart, L. (2002). *The field: The quest for the secret force of the universe.* New York, NY: Harper Perennial.

Sanders, M. (2007). *Nearing death awareness: A guide to the language, visions, and dreams of the dying.* London, UK: Jessica Kingsley.

Schwartz, G. (2002). *The afterlife experiments: Breakthrough scientific evidence of life after death.* New York, NY: Atria Books.

Talbot, M. (2011). *The holographic universe: The revolutionary theory of reality.* New York, NY: Harper Books.

References

Alexander, E. (2012). *Proof of heaven: A neurosurgeon's journey into the afterlife.* New York, NY: Simon & Schuster.

Beischel, J., Boccuzzi, M., Biuso, M., & Rock, A. J. (2015). Anomalous information reception by research mediums under blinded conditions II:

Replication and extension. *EXPLORE: The Journal of Science & Healing, 11(2)*, 136–142. doi:10.1016/j.explore.2015.01.001

Brayne, S., Farnham, C., & Fenwick, P. (2006). Deathbed phenomena and their effect on a palliative care team: A pilot study. *American Journal of Hospice & Palliative Medicine, 23*(1), 17–24.

Brayne, S., Lovelace, H., & Fenwick, P. (2008). End-of-life experiences and the dying process on a Gloucestershire nursing home as reported by nurses and care assistants. *American Journal of Hospice & Palliative Medicine, 25*(3), 195–206.

Chown, M. (2012). *Ten bonkers things about the universe.* Retrieved from http://mindscapemagazine.com/2012/06/marcus-chown-on-10-bonkers -things-about-the-universe/.

Fenwick, P. (2010). Non local effects in the process of dying: Can quantum mechanics help? *NeuroQuantology, 8*(2), 155–163.

Fenwick, P., & Brayne, S. (2011). End-of-life experiences: Reaching out for compassion, communication, and connection—Meaning of deathbed visions and coincidences. *American Journal of Hospice & Palliative Medicine, 28*(1), 7–15.

Fenwick, P., Lovelace, H., & Brayne, S. (2007). End-of-life experiences and their implications for palliative care. *International Journal of Environmental Studies, 64*(3), 315–323.

Greyson, B. (2010). Seeing dead people not known to have died: "Peak in Darien" experiences. *Anthropology & Humanism, 35*(2), 159–171. doi:10.1111/j.1548–1409.2010.01064.x

Groves, R. (2009). *The American book of living and dying: Lessons in healing spiritual pain.* New York, NY: Celestial Arts.

Guggenheim, B., & Guggenheim, J. (1997). *Hello from heaven!* New York, NY: Bantam Books.

Holden, J. M. (2009). Veridical perception in near-death experiences. In J. M. Holden, B. Greyson, & D. James (Eds.), *The handbook of near-death experiences: Thirty years of investigation* (pp. 185–211). Santa Barbara, CA: Praeger/ABC-CLIO.

Houran, J. (1997). Hallucinations that comfort: Contextual mediation of deathbed visions. *Perceptual and Motor Skills, 84*(3), 1491–1504.

Kellehear, A., Pogonet, V., Mindruta-Stratan, R., & Gorelco, V. (2012). Deathbed visions from the Republic of Moldova: A content analysis of family observations. *Omega, 64*(4), 303–317.

Koch, C. (2007, October). How does consciousness happen? *Scientific American*, 76–83.

Laszlo, E. (2008). An unexplored domain of nonlocality: Toward a scientific explanation of instrumental transcommunication. *Explore, 4*(5), 321–327.

Long, J., with Perry, P. (2010). *Evidence of the afterlife: The science of near-death experiences.* New York, NY: Harper One.

Mazzarino-Willett, A. (2010). Deathbed phenomena: Its role in peaceful death and terminal restlessness. *American Journal of Hospice & Palliative Medicine, 27*(2), 127–133.

McEvoy, J., & Zarate, O. (1997). *Introducing quantum theory.* New York, NY: Totem Books.

Moody, R. *Life after life.* (1975). New York, NY: Bantam Books.

Moyer, M. (2012). Is space digital? *Scientific American, 306,* 30–36.

Muthumana, S., Kellehear, A., Kumar, S., & Moosa, F. (2010). Deathbed visions from India: A study of family observations in Northern Kerala. *Omega, 62*(2), 97–109.

Neal, M. (2012). *To heaven and back.* Colorado Springs, CO: WaterBrook Press.

Osis, K., & Haraldsson, E. (1977). *At the hour of death: What they saw.* New York, NY: Avon Books.

Parnia, S. (2006). *What happens when we die: A groundbreaking study into the nature of life and death.* Carlsbad, CA: Hay House.

Ring, K. (1980). *Life at death: A scientific investigation of the near-death experience.* New York, NY: Quill.

Scott, R. (1978). Research on deathbed experiences: Some contemporary and historical perspectives. *Parapsychology Review, 9*(1), 20–27.

van Lommel, P. (2010). *Consciousness beyond life: The science of the near-death experience.* New York, NY: Harper One.

Vedral, V. (2011). Living in a quantum world. *Scientific American, 304,* 38–43.

Wilson, I. (1987). *The after death experience: The physics of the non-physical.* New York, NY: William Morrow.

Hypnosis

AN OVERVIEW FOR COUNSELORS

Christopher M. Faiver

Counselors and other mental health professionals may have a professional interest in the uses of clinical hypnosis with their clients. Therapists in general can find hypnosis to be a potentially effective adjunct to their repertoire of counseling and psychotherapeutic techniques.

Clinical hypnosis is a methodology or set of techniques backed by some theory, but it is not a well-defined system or school of counseling or psychotherapy. Hence, hypnosis should be utilized with the same caution and care as other counseling techniques, which the counselor derives from one's basic philosophical and theoretical stance.

In terms of basic theoretical orientation, however, hypnosis is most closely associated with the psychoanalytic school developed by Sigmund Freud. Freud himself initially employed hypnosis in his therapy. However, after his authoritarian approach to hypnotic induction failed to produce results in many of his patients, he rejected hypnosis in favor of dream interpretation and free association (Gay, 1989).

Definitions and History

In 1842 Scottish physician and surgeon James Braid (1976) coined the term *hypnosis* after the Greek word for *sleep*. Braid soon discovered that this modality was far from being a sleep state and made subsequent attempts to change the term to *monoideism* (one idea), describing more accurately the trance state as involving selective attention, a form of *super concentration*. It is evident that this term did not catch on.

There are myriad definitions of hypnosis; hence, there is no one accepted definition, an absence that can present some confusion. However, most definitions would acknowledge an altered state of consciousness, a focus of attention and concentration, and increased suggestibility, as well as some physiological changes—mostly relaxation (Crasilneck & Hall, 1989).

Moreover, one should note that all hypnosis is actually self-hypnosis, because the client controls his or her own trance state. With this point in mind, one can conclude that subjects cannot get *stuck* in a trance or be made to do anything against their will, morals, or ethics. Clients are generally alert and can play an active part in trance, including interacting with the counselor.

Certainly, though, the technique that became known as hypnosis antedated Braid by many thousands of years. Moreover, its history and development are intriguing and somewhat controversial. Some theorists (Kroger, 1977) viewed hypnosis as a prehistoric, atavistic defensive state used by early humans as protection from predators, because the stillness of a trance helped them blend into their surroundings. He was alluding to the basic response system whereby a person (or other animal) who encounters a threat (such as a saber-toothed tiger) had better be able to fight—fend it off, take flight—flee from it, or freeze—blend in with the environment in an attempt not to be perceived by the predator. Examples of the freeze response include a scared rabbit or an alert and perfectly still cat. Kroger (1977) equated hypnosis with the freeze response.

In their literature, the Egyptians, Greeks, and Romans alluded to hypnosis-like phenomena. These included oracles who seemingly went into trance in order to foretell the future, *sleep temples* in which oracles practiced their art, and magical incantations—ritualized phrases used to induce trance in order to cure disease (Crasilneck & Hall, 1989; Mutter, 1998; Waterfield, 2003).

In 1776, Franz Anton Mesmer, from whom the term *Mesmerism* is derived, stated that all persons had an energy flow, which, in cases involving pathology, needed something akin to alignment. Therefore, Mesmer sought to achieve this realignment by redirecting his patients' energy flow, their *animal magnetism*. Because of his unorthodox methods, Mesmer was later discredited by a team of scientists that included Benjamin Franklin (Waterfield, 2003). This incident, as well as the linking by some of hypnosis to the occult or for use as entertainment—stage hypnosis—contributed to its falling into disrepute. To some extent it has carried this stigma to this day (Crabtree, 1993; Gauld, 1992; Gravitz & Gerton, 1984).

As noted earlier, Sigmund Freud initially utilized the technique and eventually rejected it, although near his death he seemed more accepting of it (Crabtree, 1993; Gay, 1989). The American Medical Association (AMA) accepted hypnosis in 1958 as a mode of treatment; they were soon followed by the American Psychological Association (APA) and others. However, the AMA currently does not endorse specific treatments, such as hypnosis, and hypnosis does not appear on recent APA listings of evidence-based practices for the treatment of psychological disorders (Society of Clinical Psychology, 2013). At about the time that professional associations were acknowledging hypnosis, Milton Erickson, pioneering proponent of hypnosis in the US and developer of a unique, and now widely accepted approach to psychotherapy, co-founded the American Society of Clinical Hypnosis, the most professionally accepted organization for practitioners of clinical hypnosis (Crasilneck & Hall, 1989; Kroger, 1977; Mutter, 1988; Waterfield, 2003).

Methods of Induction

If one accepts the definition of hypnosis as *selective attention*, one can logically conclude that there are as many ways to induce a trance as there are things to pay attention to, whether visually, auditorily, and/or kinesthetically (Hammond, 1998). Some persons appear to be more visual in their approach to the world. That is, in their imagery they literally envision the scene, seeing the colors at the beach, looking at the ocean. Others are more auditory in their approach; they hear the calls of the sea gulls and sounds of the waves as they lap the shore. Still others feel the warmth of the sun on their backs as they note the grittiness of the sand between their toes. These *perceptual styles* are denoted in Richard Bandler and John Grinder's (1975a, 1975b) initial work on Neurolinguistic Programming (NLP), derived in part from observations of Milton Erickson (Grinder & Bandler, 1981; Lankton, 1979).

Actually, achieving a trance is the easy part; what is vital is what is done when a person is in trance. That is when the practitioner's knowledge, skill, and creativity must come in full force. Therefore, the practitioner should be steeped in counseling and psychological theory, techniques, and supervised clinical experience before utilizing clinical hypnosis with a client.

Indications and Contraindications

Hypnosis has many uses. In medicine it is employed as a substitute for anesthesia; in obstetrics it is utilized to assist with natural childbirth; medical professionals also have used it in numerous other areas including dermatology, cancer pain management, and pediatrics (August, 1961; Hartland, 1971; Kroger, 1977; Olness & Gardner, 1988; Orne, 1962; Spiegel & Spiegel, 2004; Wester & O'Grady, 1991; Wester & Smith, 1991; Wester & Sugarman, 2007). In dentistry hypnosis is useful to control bleeding and the gag reflex (Kroger, 1977). It can also be employed in the removal of such habits as smoking and overeating (Kroger, 1977; Spiegel & Spiegel, 2004; Wester & Smith, 1991).

Many athletes have attempted to improve their performance through the use of sports hypnosis (Edgette, 1998; Edgette & Rowan, 2003). Because memory is constructive, hypnosis has been employed in forensics only for recall of a perpetrator's identity or a license plate number rather than for totally accurate details of specific events (Perry, 1997). In the school setting, hypnosis has been used to treat test anxiety and separation anxiety as well as to improve study habits and concentration (Brown, Riddell, Summers, & Coffman, 1994).

In counseling and psychotherapy, hypnosis has often been found effective in the treatment of psychosis, sexual dysfunctions, depression, anxiety and stress, and anorexia (Araoz, 1982; Kroger, 1977; Orne, 1962; Spiegel & Spiegel, 2004; Wester, 1987; Wester & Smith, 1991; Yapko, 2006). Although some theorists argue that there are no contraindications for the use of hypnosis, others say that it is not indicated for use with actively psychotic clients or persons with severe mental disability because of their limited attention span (Kroger, 1977). Moreover, I do not employ hypnosis in situations where its consideration violates the client's religious belief system. Further, when a client presents with pain symptoms, hypnosis should be used only under a physician's recommendation, as the presence of pain may indicate that a medical disease should be ruled out (Hilgard & Hilgard, 1983; Patterson, 2010).

One area of use that I have found fascinating is *hypnoanalysis,* a combination of psychoanalysis with hypnosis (Brown & Fromm, 1986; Fromm, 1984). Hypnoanalysis utilizes the techniques of *age regression* and dream interpretation to resolve current problems. During age regression, the client under hypnosis is guided to an earlier period of development during which a psychological problem may have developed. While the client is in an altered state of consciousness, the problem can be explored, integrated, and repaired in a safe manner. It was while using this technique that psychiatrist Brian Weiss discovered "past-life therapy," a process he has continued to initiate with the induction of hypnosis (Weiss, 1988).

Another manner in which practitioners can utilize hypnosis is the style popularized by Milton Erickson (Erickson & Rossi, 1976, 1979; Haley, 1993a, 1993b; Lankton & Lankton, 1983; Rossi, 1980; Zeig & Geary, 2002). Although others in the field of clinical hypnosis rely upon tangible objects or sensations—such as a spot on the wall or the feel of one's heartbeat or music—to induce trance, Erickson used early memories and often created confusion in clients. In other words, Erickson had patients focus their attention inwardly on reverie, rather than on objects or sensations, and also concluded that the patient would enter trance as a defense against the confusion. He viewed involvement in memory and avoidance of confusion as indicators of a *naturalistic* trance. Patients recalling memories *were* in trance, quite naturally! While clients were in this naturally induced trance state, Erickson told therapeutic stories with a lesson—that is, metaphors—to clients as seeds for amelioration of particular issues. I cite Erickson's admonition as relevant to all counselors of whatever theoretical ilk: "Follow the client and stay out of the way!" In other words, fit the therapy to the client, not the client to the therapy.

Conclusion

Clinical hypnosis can be a valuable asset to the counselor's methodological repertoire. As with any technique or set of techniques, hypnosis should be applied with due care and consideration for the client, the presenting concern, and the counselor's comfort and skill level.

Suggested Resources

Print

Fross, G. H. (1974). *Handbook of hypnotic techniques.* South Orange, NJ: Power.

Hammond, D. C., & Elkins, G. R. (1994). *Standards of training in clinical hypnosis.* Des Plaines, IL: American Society of Clinical Hypnosis (ASCH).

Rossi, E. L. (2002). *The psychobiology of gene expression: Neuroscience and neurogenesis in hypnosis and the healing arts.* New York, NY: W. W. Norton.

Yapko, M. (2012). *Trancework: An introduction to the practice of clinical hypnosis* (4th ed.). New York, NY: Routledge.

Online

The American Journal of Clinical Hypnosis (ASCH): http://www.asch.net/Public/AmericanJournalofClinicalHypnosis/tabid/162/Default.aspx

American Psychological Association—Division 30 (Hypnosis): http://psychologicalhypnosis.com/

American Society of Clinical Hypnosis: http://www.asch.net/

The International Journal of Clinical and Experimental Hypnosis: http://ijceh.com/

The Milton Erickson Foundation: http://erickson-foundation.org/

Society for Clinical and Experimental Hypnosis: http://www.sceh.us/

References

Araoz, D. L. (1982). *Hypnosis & sex therapy.* New York, NY: Brunner/Mazel.

August, R. V. (1961). *Hypnosis in obstetrics.* New York, NY: McGraw-Hill.

Bandler, R., & Grinder, J. (1975a). *The structure of magic* (Vols. 1–2). Palo Alto, CA: Science and Behavior Books.

Bandler, R., & Grinder, J. (1975b). *Patterns of the hypnotic techniques of Milton H. Erickson, M.D.* (Vols. 1–2). Cupertino, CA: Meta.

Braid, J. (1976). *Neurypnology or the rationale of nervous sleep considered in relation with animal magnetism.* New York, NY: Arno Press.

Brown, D. P., & Fromm, E. (1986). *Hypnotherapy and hypnoanalysis.* Hillsdale, NJ: Lawrence Erlbaum Associates.

Brown, G. W., Riddell, R., Summers, D., & Coffman, B. (1994, August). *Use of hypnosis by practitioners in the school setting.* Paper presented at the annual meeting of the American Psychological Association, Los Angeles, CA.

Crabtree, A. (1993). *From Mesmer to Freud: Magnetic sleep and the roots of psychological healing.* New Haven, CT: Yale University Press.

Crasilneck, H., & Hall, J. (1989). *Clinical hypnosis: Principles and applications.* New York, NY: Grune & Stratton.

Edgette, J. H., & Rowan, T. (2003). *Winning the mind game: Using hypnosis in sport psychology.* Norwalk, CT: Crown House.

Edgette, J. S. (1998). Therapy is therapy is therapy: Brief clinical sport psychology. In W. J. Matthews & J. H. Edgette (Eds.), *Current thinking and research in brief therapy: Solutions, strategies, narratives* (Vol. 2, pp. 85–115). Philadelphia: Taylor & Francis.

Erickson, M. H., & Rossi, E. L. (1976). *Hypnotic realities: The induction of clinical hypnosis & forms of indirect suggestion.* New York, NY: Irvington.

Erickson, M. H., & Rossi, E. L. (1979). *Hypnotherapy: An exploratory casebook.* New York, NY: Irvington.

Fromm, E. (1984). The theory and practice of hypnoanalysis. In W.C. Wester, II & A. H. Smith, Jr. (Eds.), *Clinical hypnosis: A multidisciplinary approach* (pp. 142–154). New York, NY: J. B. Lippincott.

Gauld, A. (1992). *A history of hypnotism.* Cambridge, UK: Cambridge University Press.

Gay, P. (Ed.). (1989). *The Freud reader.* New York, NY: Norton.

Gravitz, M. A., & Gerton, M. I. (1984). Origins of the term "hypnotism" prior to Braid. *American Journal of Clinical Hypnosis, 27,* 107–110.

Grinder, J., & Bandler, R. (1981). *Trance-formations: NLP & the structure of hypnosis.* Moab, UT: Real People Press.

Hammond, D. C. (Ed.). (1998). *Hypnotic induction and suggestion: An introductory manual.* Des Plaines, IL: American Society of Clinical Hypnosis.

Haley, J. (1993a). *Jay Haley on Milton E. Erickson.* New York, NY: Brunner/Mazel.

Haley, J. (1993b). *Uncommon therapy: The psychiatric techniques of Milton Erickson* (2nd ed.). New York, NY: Norton.

Hartland, J. (1971). *Medical and dental hypnosis and its clinical applications* (2nd ed.). London, UK: Bailliere Tindall.

Hilgard, E. R., & Hilgard, J. R. (1983). *Hypnosis in the relief of pain* (Rev. ed.). Los Altos, CA: William Kaufmann.

Kroger, W. (1977). *Clinical and experimental hypnosis in medicine, dentistry, and psychology* (2nd ed.). Philadelphia, PA: J. B. Lippincott.

Lankton, S. (1979). *Practical magic: The clinical applications of Neuro-Linguistic Programming.* Cupertino, CA: Meta.

Lankton, S. R., & Lankton, C. H. (1983). *The answer within: A clinical framework of Ericksonian hypnotherapy.* New York, NY: Brunner/Mazel.

Mutter, C. (1998). The history of hypnosis. In D. C. Hammond (Ed.), *Hypnotic induction and suggestion: An introductory manual* (pp. 10–12). Des Plaines, IL: American Society of Clinical Hypnosis.

Olness, K., & Gardner, G. G. (1988). *Hypnosis and hypnotherapy with children* (2nd ed.). Philadelphia, PA: Grune & Stratton.

Orne, M. T. (1962). Medical uses of hypnosis. *Group for the Advancement of Psychiatry, 8,* 641–708.

Patterson, D. (2010). *Clinical hypnosis for pain control.* Washington, DC: American Psychological Association.

Perry, C. (1997). Admissibility and per se exclusion of hypnotically elicited recall in American courts of law. *International Journal of Clinical and Experimental Hypnosis, 45*(3), 266–279.

Rossi, E. L. (Ed.). (1980). *The collected papers of Milton H. Erickson, M.D.,* Volumes I–IV. New York, NY: Irvington.

Society of Clinical Psychology. (2013). *Psychological treatments.* Retrieved from http://www.div12.org/psychological-treatments/treatments/

Spiegel, H., & Spiegel, D. (2004). *Trance and treatment: Clinical uses of hypnosis.* Washington, DC: American Psychiatric Association.

Waterfield, R. (2003). *Hidden depths: The story of hypnosis.* New York, NY: Brunner-Routledge.

Weiss, B. (1988). *Many lives, many masters: The true story of a prominent psychiatrist, his young patient, and the past-life therapy that changed both their lives.* New York, NY: Simon & Schuster.

Wester, W. C. (Ed.). (1987). *Clinical hypnosis: A case management approach.* Cincinnati, OH: Behavioral Science Center.

Wester, W. C., & O'Grady, D. J. (1991). *Clinical hypnosis with children.* New York, NY: Brunner/Mazel.

Wester, W., & Smith, A. (1991). *Clinical hypnosis: A multidisciplinary approach.* Philadelphia, PA: J. B. Lippincott.

Wester II, W. C., & Sugarman, L. I. (Eds). (2007). *Therapeutic hypnosis with children and adolescents.* Norwalk, CT: Crown House.

Yapko, M. D. (Ed). (2006). *Hypnosis and treating depression: Applications in clinical practice.* New York, NY: Routledge/Taylor & Francis.

Zeig, J., & Geary, B. (2002). *The handbook of Ericksonian hypnosis and psychotherapy.* Phoenix, AZ: Milton H. Erickson Foundation Press.

Intercessory Prayer

Allen H. Weber

Can humans communicate with God or powers greater than themselves? How do we know when there is no physical evidence to verify such communication? Can such communication affect our material world and produce positive results or healing? Most people seem to think so (Callahan, 2000). Belief in the possibility and effectiveness of prayer, as dialogue with God or with spiritual beings, is a staple of most religious traditions (Byrd, 1988). For example, even a cursory reading of the Bible, the scriptural cornerstone of the Judaeo-Christian tradition, reveals as its central theme the notion of a personal God who is deeply involved in the lives of human beings and who regularly engages in communication with them (Anonymous, 2005).

Whereas the God of the Bible requires adoration or worship, several other prayer forms are also encouraged, including thanksgiving for God's mercy and goodness and petitionary prayer based on confidence in God's power to intervene in a positive way in people's lives (Anonymous, 2005). Based on that same confidence and the belief that God relates both to individuals as well as with individuals gathered in community, people are encouraged to pray for one another (Callahan, 2000). During the early history of Christianity, Christians came to believe in the communion of saints, or the bonding of all who have died in the friendship of God with the living faithful (Mahoney, 2002). In this context, praying for one another becomes a process of interceding before God for the welfare of another. According to Mahoney (2002) the word *intercede* derives from a combination of two Latin words meaning one who goes between and reconciles two parties. The one interceding, somewhat in the manner of an attorney in court, pleads for mercy on behalf of the party in need. Thus, to offer intercession is to plead for the benefit of someone else (Mahoney, 2002)

Since the appearance of human self-consciousness, human beings have likely engaged in some form of communication with deities or transcendent powers (Harris et al., 1999). The development of reflective self-consciousness revealed the presence of natural forces and events over which humans experienced little or no control (Byrd, 1988). Thus, primarily for protection and to heal their wounds and illnesses, humans sought ways to encounter, appease, and engage the mysterious powers they believed controlled the events over which they felt helpless (Byrd, 1988). As a result, special individuals or healers arose in other societies who were specialists in contacting and engaging these divine powers (Mahoney, 2002). These healers, with their incantations, prayers, and rituals, were perhaps the first to engage in intercessory prayer as a healing rite. Eventually, this practice has become a part of all of the major world religions and many primitive faiths as well. Although there appears to be a dearth of in-depth study of this phenomenon and very little empirical research, the practice and effectiveness of this form of healing is widely supported through anecdotal reports.

For a long time and for various reasons, including the division between empirical science and religion since the Enlightenment, the medical profession and the counseling and therapy professions have avoided the topic of intercessory prayer, considering it unscientific and leaving it to theologians and pastors for discussion (Byrd, 1988; Townsend, Kladder, Ayele, & Mulligan, 2002). Recently, it appears this unwillingness of science to study the possible effectiveness of intercessory prayer has somewhat lessened (Byrd, 1988; Harris et al., 1999; Townsend et al., 2002). Yet even theologians are not unanimous in believing that prayer can affect biological reality. In an article supporting the practice of intercessory prayer, Sidney Callahan (2000) noted the theological caution on the part of some people who assert that, at most, one can change one's consciousness and attitude towards the divine will but cannot actually change material reality.

Notwithstanding the many issues and problems surrounding research on the effectiveness of intercessory prayer, two landmark studies were undertaken (Byrd, 1988; Harris et al., 1999), and the second of the two (Harris et al., 1999) represented an attempt to replicate and improve on the first (Byrd, 1988). Indeed, these studies are the foundation of most if not all of the scientific data on this subject to date. It is possible to study the effects of intercessory prayer in two ways. Unknown to the subject, a subject can be prayed for at a distance; and in the other case, one can be aware of the fact that people are praying on one's behalf. Researchers have studied the former of these two situations (Byrd, 1988; Harris et al., 1999). In the latter case, because the individual is aware of the prayers, it is difficult to separate the placebo effect from the effect of prayer, thus rendering results difficult to evaluate.

Townsend et al. (2002) reviewed five randomly controlled trials designed to determine the effectiveness of intercessory prayer. Three of the five trials were statistically significant. Despite major limitations, one study examining whether Protestant prayer influenced healing for children with leukemia suggested reduced mortality among these patients (Harris et al., 1999). Harris and colleagues (1999) conducted an important double-blind study with 393 coronary care patients to examine the effect of intercessory prayer, using randomized assignment to a prayer group and a control group. Evangelical Christians prayed for members of the treatment group daily until the conclusion of their hospital stay. Despite limitations of the study, results suggested significant health benefits accrued to members of the treatment group. Harris et al. (1999) attempted to replicate Byrd's (1988) study in a double-blind study of 990 patients admitted to a coronary care unit over the period of one year. The overall objective was to determine whether intercessory prayer reduced the duration of hospital stays and serious medical problems. Patients were randomly assigned to a control or a treatment group. Teams of five Christians of varied denominations prayed daily for group members using only the member's first name. Results suggested a 10% better outcome for members of the treatment group. Overall, despite limitations of these and other more general studies on prayer's beneficial effect on health, the reviewers concluded that a preponderance of evidence supports religion's beneficial effect on health, while calling for more studies (Townsend et al., 2002). The reviewers did not address the question of a causal mechanism that might be involved in intercessory prayer.

Many physicians and researchers remain skeptical. Some questions arise from the obvious methodological difficulties. Others go to the heart of serious philosophical problems. Kelly (2002), for example, questioned if prayer is applied to patients in the same way as medicine. How does one decide the "dosage," i.e., how often should prayers be offered? Several other complex methodological issues have been raised as well. For example, what should be the desired outcome? Kelly gave the example of a person in a vegetative state following a stroke. Should one pray for the best outcome, which might be for the person to die? She and others raised serious questions about the intersection of science and metaphysics. Science deals with the material world, the concrete. Metaphysics and theology, however, deal with other forms of ultimate reality that cannot be measured effectively. Ultimately, there are no effective answers to this question, and there probably never will be; prayer involves another being, a supernatural entity shrouded in mystery. Most believers in the power of intercessory prayer would also support the use of the best medical science (Callahan, 2000; Kelly, 2002).

As the above studies indicate, prayer should be an adjunct to healing rather than an exclusive method (Kelly, 2002). Indeed, if God is believed to be the source of all being, then the use of the techniques developed by medical science would be complementary to intercession. Finally, there are different ways for a person to experience healing (Callahan, 2000; Kelly, 2002). Sometimes there is an actual physical cure or change in condition; often and more common is a spiritual strengthening that has a holistic effect on the person's overall health.

What about the ethical questions involved? Gundersen (2000) asked if religion could be harmful to patients. Experts are divided on this question. Sloan, for example, believed that "patients may be made to feel guilty or 'insufficiently faithful'" (quoted in Gundersen, 2000, p. 171). Many physicians believe that religion does have a place in medicine; others believe either that physicians should stay away from an area not their expertise or that use of religion could inappropriately influence a patient's beliefs (Gundersen, 2000).

Because all of this research has primarily been conducted with patients with medical conditions, what about psychotherapy clients? Should the counselor incorporate intercessory prayer into treatment? The use of intercessory prayer for an outcome determined to be best for the client can do no harm if the praying is unknown to the client. On the other hand, the therapist should not engage in such prayer with a client who is not open to the experience. To do so would be unethical practice. Also, in working with a client who requests intercessory prayers, a counselor uncomfortable with the prayer could engage family members, friends, and others comfortable with the approach.

Conclusion

The practice of using intercessory prayer has been associated with human healing for most of human history. It has long been believed by a majority of human beings to be an effective method of healing (Byrd, 1988). Though there is a lack of scientific evidence to support its effectiveness, recent interest and several investigations on the part of physicians and scientists seem to suggest that there are benefits in using intercessory prayer as an adjunct to other methods of healing (Byrd, 1988; Harris et al., 1999; Townsend et al., 2002). Nonetheless, the evidence is not compelling, and many methodological, theological, and ethical questions remain unanswered. However, if there is no potential for harm, and if practiced ethically in the best interest of clients, intercessory prayer should be considered as an optional additional technique that professional counselors and therapists may employ.

Suggested Resources

Print

Murray, A. (2003). *The ministry of intercessory prayer.* Grand Rapids, MI: Bethany House.

Sheets, D. (1996). *How God can use your prayers to move heaven and earth.* Ventura, CA: Gospel Light.

References

Anonymous. (2005). The Catholic holy Bible, new American Bible. In Anonymous (Author), *Bible* (pp. 1–1475). Charlotte, NC: Saint Benedict Press.

Byrd, R. C. (1988). Positive therapeutic effects of intercessory prayer in a coronary care unit population. *Southern Medical Journal, 81*(7), 826–829.

Callahan, S. (2000, April 21). Prayer makes a difference. *Commonweal, 127,* 7.

Gundersen, L. (2000). Faith and healing. *Annals of Internal Medicine, 132*(2), 169–172.

Harris, W. S., Gowda, M., Kolb, J. W., Strychacz, C. P., Vacek, J. L., Jones, P. G., . . . McAllister, B. D. (1999). A randomized, controlled trial of the effects of remote, intercessory prayer on outcomes in patients admitted to the coronary care unit. *Archives of Internal Medicine, 159,* 2273–2278.

Kelly, A. L. (2002, December). Prayer in a petri dish? *Health,* 46–49.

Mahoney, P. J. (2002). Intercession. In T. Carson (Ed.), *New Catholic encyclopedia* (2nd ed., pp. 519–520). Washington, DC: Catholic University of America.

Townsend, M., Kladder, V., Ayele, H., & Mulligan, T. (2002). Systematic review of clinical trials examining the effects of religion on health. *Southern Medical Journal, 95,* 1429–1434.

Labyrinths

AN INTRODUCTION

Michele L. Kielty

 According to Johnson (2001), a labyrinth is an ancient symbol that promotes finding wholeness via a purposeful path. The purpose of the labyrinth is to act as a spiritual tool in awakening participants to a unifying connection to self, others, and the light within (Artress, 1995). Usually, labyrinths are circular patterns that have a single path that leads to the center and back out. There is only one path, and one cannot get lost while traversing a labyrinth, as one could while navigating a maze. Labyrinths are large enough to be walked on, and individuals using labyrinths are meant to gain spiritual insight as they walk slowly in a meditative stance (Plugge & McCormick, 1997). Labyrinths are often made of canvas, tile, brick, or fabric, but they also can be etched in grassy areas, on coins, on pottery, and even on sand.

The horizontal path of the labyrinth is meant to remind individuals of the strong divine connection that can take place on a horizontal plane through connections to self, others, and the Divine, rather than through a vertical, hierarchical path that may foster isolation (Artress, 1995). Labyrinths are designed to help establish a balance between the mind and the body and to foster harmony between the psychological and physical selves through a spiritual awakening experience (Dunphy, Borsdorf, & Chambliss, 2000).

Currently, labyrinths are used as spiritual tools for relaxation and meditation. They have recently been used by members of religious groups, by hyperactive children, by medical patients employing alternative therapies, by Alzheimer's patients, and at spiritual retreat centers. Today, labyrinths are being used in many cultures for walking meditation, stress management, and spiritual development (Dunphy et al., 2000). In addition to their current use, labyrinths have a long and rich history.

History of Labyrinths

Labyrinths have been in existence for over 4,000 years, and they are now found in most of the world's religions (Dunphy et al., 2000). It is thought that labyrinths have always been used in a spiritual manner throughout the history of civilization (Johnson, 2006). The oldest classical labyrinth is known as the seven-circuit labyrinth—as seen in the picture at the beginning of this chapter—that evolved from a spiral figure in nature. These labyrinths were printed on coins in ancient civilizations. Labyrinths have been found across cultures in practices as diverse as the Jewish Kabbala mystical tradition, the Hopi medicine wheel, Tibetan paintings and mandalas, Syrian ceramic vessels, and Greek clay tablets (Artress, 1995).

The labyrinth seemed to disappear from usage prior to the Middle Ages but then re-emerged as a form of spiritual pilgrimage in the Catholic Church. It then seemed to drop out of public awareness for about 350 years until Lauren Artress, an Episcopalian Canon, brought it back into use (Plugge & McCormick, 1997). Artress (1995) started the Worldwide Labyrinth Project whose "mission it is to reintroduce the labyrinth into churches, retreat centers, hospitals, prisons, parks, airports, and community spaces throughout the world to promote spiritual healing" (pp. 4–5).

The eleven-circuit labyrinth that is used most often today can be found at the Chartres Cathedral in France, as well as at Grace Cathedral in San Francisco, California, where Lauren Artress manages the Labyrinth Project. The eleven-circuit labyrinth was devised during the early Gothic era. It is geometrically balanced and is based on a thirteen-point star. The center of the labyrinth is called the rosette, resembling a flower with six petals and representing the six days of creation or the six stages of planetary evolution. Individuals enter from the left and travel clockwise (Plugge & McCormick, 1997). Many individuals assert that in the past, the labyrinth served as a calendar in which the four quadrants represented the four seasons of the year. Churches may have used this calendar to determine the timing of Easter (Artress, 1995).

Applicable Research

Unfortunately, very little research has been published on the topic of labyrinths. Most of the benefits of labyrinths are anecdotal in nature because the phenomenological experience of the labyrinth is difficult to measure and validate. However, Dunphy et al. (2000) recently completed a study to assess the effectiveness of the labyrinth as a wellness tool. Participants were an experimental group whose members individually walked the eleven-circuit labyrinth and a control group whose members participated in focus-walking on a basketball court. The sample size was small and limited to a college population. The researchers found no significant differences between the groups on the pre- and post-test wellness questionnaire. However, between group *t* test results on individual post-test items "revealed a trend indicating that labyrinth group members reported feeling more 'balanced' than did control group members after their walking experiences" (p. 15).

Because the labyrinth is a spiritual tool that has had a recent resurgence in use, the field of possibilities for future research seems open. Researchers interested in studying labyrinths may want to examine the effects of labyrinth walking on various kinds of psychological and spiritual measures for a variety of populations, such as at-risk youth, hospital patients, religious persons, and various counseling/psychotherapy group members.

Indications and Contraindications

Counselors wishing to use labyrinths as a tool for their clients may want to keep several issues in mind. First, it is important to recognize that the benefits of labyrinth walking are currently purely anecdotal; thus, counselors cannot assert that there are any proven benefits of such a practice. An additional caution is to help clients to avoid unrealistic expectations of the labyrinth experience such as, "This experience will take away my difficult feelings," or "This practice will heal my illness." Finally, Dunphy et al. (2000) noted that first-time labyrinth walkers may experience anxiety or fear about both their potential affective responses to the experience and the possible results of the walk. It is important that individuals use the labyrinth in a way that feels most comfortable for them. For example, some clients may choose to go slowly, others will walk fast, and some may even skip or crawl (Grace Cathedral, n.d.).

Counselors and clients who choose to utilize the ancient labyrinth-walking practice may experience various benefits. According to Plugge and McCormick (1997), "the labyrinth is an ideal place to ask our most puzzling or pertinent life questions" (p. 7). Walking the labyrinth allows people's souls to quiet and motivates them to engage in a calming, meditative walking experience. The same authors noted that using a labyrinth may stimulate interest in fields of study such as philosophy, music, mythology, language, and astronomy.

West (2000) identified specific uses for the labyrinth that may be applicable to clients in various circumstances. First, clients may use the time during the labyrinth walk to focus on a specific intention or prayer or to work on a particular emotion. For example, a client dealing with anger associated with a relationship change may focus on healing the hurt behind the anger as a specific intention for his or her walk. Clients also can de-stress and take the focus off worries related to illness, work, or relationship problems by surrendering their worries to a divine power during the labyrinth walk. They also may ask for inspiration and guidance during the meditative walk in order to better handle an issue of concern. West noted that some individuals may use their time during the labyrinth walk to celebrate a life passage, to focus on gratitude, to ask for creative inspiration, or to ask for guidance on a vocational concern. West suggested that, if appropriate, individuals in conflict can ask the other party to walk the labyrinth with them to symbolize the start of a healing journey. Finally, West stated that, for some individuals, walking a labyrinth while focusing on a specific affirmation such as, "I am an open channel for creativity to flow through" (p. 147) might be especially helpful.

One suggestion for clients and/or counselors who use the labyrinth as a spiritual tool is to keep in mind the three-fold journey of labyrinth walking as defined by Artress (1995). Artress asserted that walking from the beginning to the center of the labyrinth symbolizes *purgation*: purging barriers to the divine and quietly surrendering the self. The second stage of the journey is *illumination*: when the walker reaches the center and receives an insight related to one's focus. Finally, the third stage, *union*, is when the sojourner walks back out to the entrance following the same path, and integrates insight(s) into the life to which one is returning. Walkers may wish to walk into the labyrinth with their palms facing down to symbolize a centering of the self and walk out with palms facing up to indicate reception (Johnson, 2006).

I found in the literature no contraindications related to utilizing labyrinths. However, heeding the aforementioned cautions may be useful. For example, staying attuned to one's level of anxiety about and/ or expectations of the labyrinth experience may ameliorate potentially overwhelming or negative experiences. Because labyrinths can have many twists and turns along the route, walkers may wish to use caution while traveling the labyrinth. Finally, individuals with physical disabilities could find it difficult to enter and/or navigate the labyrinth.

Conclusion

Labyrinths are ancient symbols that can be used as spiritual tools for growth, centering, surrender, and insight. They serve to keep one centered and connected to self, others, and a divine energy through horizontal relatedness. Although there is a lack of scientific research to support the benefits of labyrinth-walking, anecdotal reports indicate that clients in various life situations may experience benefits from the practice. These benefits include calmness, clarity, insight, and a sense of connection through a meditative walking experience.

Suggested Resources

Print

Occhiogrosso, P. (1991). *Through the labyrinth: Stories of the search for spiritual transformation in everyday life.* New York, NY: Viking.

Online

Earth Symbols Labyrinth Builder: http://www.earthsymbols.com/
Labyrinth Enterprises: http://www.labyrinthproject.com

References

Artress, L. (1995). *Walking a sacred path: Rediscovering the labyrinth as a spiritual tool.* New York, NY: Riverhead Books.
Dunphy, M., Borsdorf, L., & Chambliss, C. (2000). *Educational applications of wellness techniques: An experimental investigation of the effects of labyrinth walking* (Report No. ED440300). Collegeville, PA: Ursinus College. Retrieved from ERIC database (ED440300).

Ferre, R. D. (1996). *The labyrinth revival.* St. Louis, MO: One Way Press.

Grace Cathedral. (n.d.). The Cathedral labyrinths. Retrieved from http://www.gracecathedral.org/labyrinth/

Johnston, D. (2001). *Lessons for living: Simple solutions for life's problems.* Macon, GA: Dagali Press.

Johnston, D. (2006). The labyrinth. Retrieved from http://www.lessons4living.com/labyrinth/htm

Plugge, C., & McCormick, D. (1997). *Walking a path of transformation: Using the labyrinth as a spiritual tool* (Report No. ED414144). Retrieved from ERIC database (ED414144).

West, M. G. (2000). *Exploring the labyrinth: A guide for healing and spiritual growth.* New York, NY: Broadway Books.

Meditation

Tracey E. Robert

Meditation is a spiritual practice that has existed for thousands of years, often associated with Eastern religions. Meditation has existed as a religious practice and a secular tradition. Research studies documenting its psychological, physiological, and transpersonal benefits have been increasing over the past 40 years. Since the 1960s, meditation has existed as a spiritual intervention and strategy in the practice of counseling to alleviate or lessen a variety of mental, emotional, and physical problems (Holzel, Lazar, Gard, Schuman-Olivier, Vago, & Ott, 2011; Kelly, 1995; Shapiro & Walsh, 2003). The integration of meditation into clinical practice, both in counseling and the medical field, has seen growth since the 1980s (Baer, 2003). However, its increasing use as an alternative therapy in medicine and as part of the counseling process has stressed the nonreligious nature of the intervention. Both the medical model and the counseling practice have focused on the integrative health benefit of treating the body, mind, and spirit.

The use of meditation in counseling has been described as an opportunity to offer clients a tool to increase awareness and facilitate a mind-body-spirit balance (Greason, 2011). Three types of meditation have been described in the literature: (a) devotional meditation (contemplative prayer) that is often associated with Christian traditions; (b) concentrative meditation in which one focuses on something, such as attending visually to a candle, repeating a mantra, or attending to one's own breathing; and (c) mindfulness meditation in which one becomes aware of present experience by noticing feelings, thoughts, and sensations with acceptance and without judgment as they arise to freely flow through the mind (Burkhardt & Nagai-Jacobson, 2002; Faiver, Ingersoll, O'Brien, & McNally, 2001; Young, DeLorenzi, & Cunningham, 2011). Meditators become increasingly aware of both internal and external experiences occurring in the moment connecting soul, spirit, mind, and body.

Definition/Description and History of the Intervention

Beginning in the 1960s with the popularity of transcendental meditation—a kind of concentrative meditation—the incorporation of meditation into the counseling process has been growing and developing. The typical definition of meditation, concentrative or mindful, is that it involves the regulation of attention while concentrating on the present and that it requires an openness and acceptance of the experience (Holzel et al., 2011; Kabat-Zinn, 1990).

In the 1970s, medical researchers at the University of Massachusetts Medical Center, under the direction of Jon Kabat-Zinn, explored the idea of training cardiac patients in a stress reduction clinic using mindfulness meditation techniques (MBSR). The reduction in hypertension and improved cardiac health led Kabat-Zinn to share this technique with Herbert Benson at Harvard Medical Center. Benson (2000) developed the relaxation response using meditation techniques to work with patients referred with stress-induced illnesses such as hypertension, arthritis, insomnia, depression, and cancer. This activity eventually led to the development of what is now the Benson-Henry Institute for Mind Body Medicine at Massachusetts General Hospital, where patients and medical personnel are trained in meditation and relaxation techniques.

Both Kabat-Zinn and Benson's techniques focus on the breath. The belief is that breath plays a fundamental role in healing. It is viewed as a vital life force, a life rhythm, and the ebb and flow of energy in a person's body. It is the bridge between the mind and the body as it anchors awareness of one's body. Paying attention to breathing enables a meditator to feel its calming nature and the force of life. It allows the person to connect with one's full being by simply noticing the flow of breath and accepting feelings in the present moment. The calmness that comes with breathing mindfully enables a person to develop a sense of stability and an inner peace. The breath has also been described as the embodiment of the spirit (Chandler, Holden, & Kolander, 1992). The potential for meditation to provide healing interventions (Baer, 2003) has increased the integration of this intervention into the counseling process.

Indications

The above meditation practices have been used in individual and group counseling sessions with clients across the lifespan in a variety of settings including schools, hospitals, clinics, and private practice. The integration of these practices expands both clients' and counselors' coping skills, such as regulation of emotions, anger management, increased concentrative focus, and reduction of stress, and this process can also tap into the spiritual domain.

The use of meditation as a method of relaxation and an effective tool in managing stress, chronic illness, addictions, anxiety, and health problems has been demonstrated (Baer, 2003). It must be done on a regular basis and as a practice in order for it to yield long-term benefit. It requires commitment and the scheduling of regular practice (Greason, 2011). This action demonstrates the value of the practice to the client and therefore increases the benefit. The intention to meditate is vital to the effectiveness of the intervention (Kabat-Zinn, 1994).

Physical benefits are relaxation, increased concentration, and slowing of breathing and heart rate that can lead to lower blood pressure and metabolic rate; decrease in chronic pain, hypertension, anxiety, blood glucose levels, and stress; and enhancement of overall immune system functioning. Psychological benefits are enhanced mental alertness and creativity, improved memory, and an increased sense of self-awareness, self-compassion, and joy. Spiritual benefits include a sense of peace and wellbeing and a connection with inner peace and spirit.

Cautions and Contraindications

There are contraindications for use of meditation with certain client populations. Multiculturally competent counselors should be sensitive to clients' varying belief systems and their view of meditation before recommending it to them.

The use of meditation may result in altered perceptions and feelings of lack of grounding. Therefore, it is not recommended for use with clients who have diagnoses of chronic schizophrenia and dissociative disorders or trauma histories (Chandler et al., 1992). Caution is recommended when using meditation with clients presenting a history of trauma or abuse. Nonetheless, spiritual interventions, particularly meditation, have been used very effectively with sexually abused clients (Gange-Fling, Veach, Kuang, & Houg, 2000). In addition, practical pitfalls include environmental conditions such as outside noise, time, cell phones, and personal interruptions (Kabat-Zinn, 2003).

Conclusion

An increase in interest in and use of meditation as an intervention in medical and counseling practice has expanded the tools available for counselors and clients alike. Training and education in methods and techniques are growing as public awareness increases through Internet resources and publications. Research studies continue to be developed and are encouraged by the medical community and government agencies such as the Veterans Administration and their integration of mindfulness in PTSD treatment. The cost effective benefits are made apparent.

Suggested Resources

Online

The Benson-Henry Institute for Mind Body Medicine: http://www
    .bensonhenryinstitute.org/
Center for Mindfulness in Medicine, Health Care, and Society at the
    University of Massachusetts Medical School: http://www.umassmed.edu/
    cfm/contact/index.aspx
Meditation Society of America: http://www.meditationsociety.com
Meditation Infocenter in HolisticOnline.com: http://www.1stholistic.com/
    Meditation
Daniel Siegel, Author of *Mindsight*: http://drdansiegel.com/
UCLA Mindful Awareness Research Center: http://marc.ucla.edu/

References

Baer, R. (2003). Mindfulness training as a clinical intervention: A conceptual
    and empirical review. *Clinical Psychology: Science and Practice, 10*,
    125–143.
Benson, H. (2000). *The relaxation response.* New York, NY: Harper.
Burkhardt, M. A., & Nagai-Jacobson, M. G. (2002). *Spirituality: Living our
    connectedness.* Albany, NY: Delmar.
Chandler, C. K., Holden, J. M., & Kolander, C. A. (1992). Counseling
    for spiritual wellness: Theory and practice. *Journal of Counseling &
    Development, 71*, 168–175.
Faiver, C., Ingersoll, R. E., O'Brien, E., & McNally, C. (2001). *Explorations in
    counseling and spirituality.* Belmont, CA: Wadsworth.

Gange-Fling, M., Veach, P. M., Kuang, H., & Houg, B. (2000). Effects of childhood sexual abuse on client spiritual well-being. *Counseling and Values, 44*(2), 84–91.

Greason, P. (2011). Mindfulness. In C. S. Cashwell & J. S. Young (Eds.), *Integrating spirituality and religion into counseling: A guide to competent practice* (pp. 183–208). Alexandria, VA: American Counseling Association.

Holzel, B. K., Lazar, S. W., Gard, T., Schuman-Olivier, Z., Vago, D. R., & Ott, U. (2011). How does mindfulness meditation work? Proposing mechanisms of action from a conceptual and neural perspective. *Psychological Science, 6*, 537–559.

Kabat-Zinn, J. (1990). *Full catastrophe living: Using the wisdom of your body and mind to face stress, pain, and illness.* New York, NY: Delacorte.

Kabat-Zinn, J. (1994). *Wherever you go: There you are.* New York, NY: Hyperion.

Kabat-Zinn, J. (2003). Mindfulness-based interventions in context: Past, present, and future. *Clinical Psychology: Science & Practice, 10*, 144–156.

Kelly, E. W. (1995). *Spirituality and religion in counseling and psychotherapy: Diversity in theory and practice.* Alexandria, VA: American Counseling Association.

Shapiro, S. L., & Walsh. R. (2003). An analysis of recent meditation research and suggestions for future directions. *Humanistic Psychologist, 31*, 86–114.

Young, M. E., DeLorenzi, L. D., & Cunningham, L. (2011). Using meditation in addiction counseling. *Journal of Addictions & Offender Counseling, 32*, 58–70.

Mindfulness Practice

Craig S. Cashwell
Jodi L. Tangen

Breathing in, I calm body and mind.
Breathing out, I smile.
Dwelling in the present moment
I know this is the only moment.

—Thich Nhat Hanh (1987)

The mind is a busy place. According to L'Amour, "Few of us ever live in the present. We are forever anticipating what is to come or remembering what has gone" (L'Amour, n.d., para. 9). To illustrate this point further, consider a typical day. You wake up and make a lengthy list of tasks that need to be accomplished for the day. Of course, the list is much longer than you can possibly complete. As you try to move through these tasks, you feel some anxiety because you are behind. You try to focus on a task, but your email beeps and you respond; later your phone rings, and you interrupt your work to answer it. All the while, you feel a tightness in your stomach to which you do not attend, knowing at some level that it is the unfinished business of an argument that you had with your partner the day before and deciding, on some level, that you do not have time to deal with it right now. Random thoughts come and go throughout the day. At day's end, you are not sure what you have accomplished, as your list of tasks is longer than it was at the beginning of the day. You spend time at night ruminating about how much you will have to accomplish tomorrow. Such is the way of the *monkey mind*, always leaping from one place to the next, moving quickly with little, if any, time to be still and quiet. As Gunaratana (2002) noted, "The reason we are all stuck in life's mud is that we ceaselessly run from our problems and after our desires" (p. 97). A practice that helps remedy the waywardness of *monkey mind* is mindfulness.

Definition and History of Mindfulness

The focus of this chapter is mindfulness, or *vipassana,* practice. The most basic premise of this discussion is that mindfulness meditation is not simply about sitting quietly in the lotus position for hours. Rather, mindfulness is a *way of life* that is cultivated through a disciplined meditation practice. Mindfulness is about being alive and awake to what is occurring in the current moment. According to Kabat-Zinn (1994), mindfulness is characterized by an intentional endeavor to pay attention to the present moment without judgment. Unencumbered (or at least less encumbered) by fears of the future or ruminations on the past, the mind is quieter, more at peace, and more fully alive. Thich Nhat Hanh (1976) captured this idea by describing the practice of washing dishes.

> There are two ways to wash the dishes. The first is to wash the dishes in order to have clean dishes, and the second is to wash the dishes in order to wash the dishes . . . If while washing dishes, we think only of the cup of tea that awaits us, thus hurrying to get the dishes out of the way as if they were a nuisance . . . we are not alive during the time we are washing the dishes. (p. 4)

Similarly, as Welwood (2000) stated, the aim of mindfulness practice is "full participation in life, but *conscious* participation, rather than the unconscious participation of pre-reflective identification. What finally replaces divided consciousness is pure presence" (p. 112). Mindfulness is nonjudgmental observation. You cannot observe something fully if you are expending energy denying its existence.

The path of mindfulness is cultivated through the practice of *vipassana* (or insight) meditation, a clear awareness of what is happening as it is happening. Mindfulness is cultivated through the balanced development of insight and concentration. Concentration meditation, or *samatha,* is a state in which the mind is focused on one item, such as the breath, and not allowed to wander. When this occurs, both mind and body experience a pervasive quietness and calmness. Gunaratana (2002) likened the mind to a cup of muddy water. Only by keeping the cup still will the mud settle down so that the water can be seen more clearly. Thus, it is necessary to cultivate concentration and insight in a balanced manner. Concentration without insight allows the mud to settle, but without an awareness of the new clarity. Efforts at insight without concentration result in a continuation of our "muddy" awareness stemming from our denial of the negative in our lives and pursuit of the positive. Such awareness is the awareness of illusion.

Vipassana meditation uses the tool of concentration to erode the illusions of the ego-mind and allows a gradual process of increasing awareness to occur. This spiritual practice has developed out of 2,500 years of practice within the highly traditional cultures of South and Southeast Asia. Though derived as the primary practice of Buddhism, vipassana meditation has applications to clients from a diverse range of belief systems. For those who want practice without beliefs, both vipassana and samatha meditation may be framed as stress management techniques. Though relaxation is a key component of meditation, vipassana meditation seeks the further goal of present-moment awareness. Not only can mindfulness be used within the context of multiple belief systems, it can also be used from multiple theoretical lenses.

Theoretical Foundation and Research

Mindfulness has been integrated into many therapeutic interventions (e.g., Mindfulness-Based Stress Reduction [MBSR; Kabat-Zinn, 1982], Mindfulness-Based Cognitive Therapy [MBCT; Segal, Williams, & Teasdale, 2002], Dialectical Behavior Therapy [DBT; Linehan, 1993], and Acceptance and Commitment Therapy [ACT; Hayes, Strosahl, & Wilson, 1999]). As such, it is an adaptable intervention and can be effectively integrated into many theoretical orientations.

Abundant literature surrounds mindfulness and counseling. According to Baer (2010), mindfulness reduces distress by decentering thoughts, promoting self-compassion, regulating emotions, structurally changing the brain, promoting psychological flexibility, encouraging values identification, enhancing spirituality, and increasing attention and memory skills. Other benefits include increased oxygen intake, relaxation, slowed heart rate, reduced stress, better immune system functioning, and slowed aging processes (Parnell, 2002). Furthermore, anecdotal benefits include the cultivation of inner strength, insight, peace of mind, silence, greater appreciation and wonder, relaxation, self-healing, and pleasure (Parnell, 2002). After an exhaustive review of research supporting the use of mindfulness, Greason (2011) simply stated, "Mindfulness alleviates suffering" (p. 190).

Practice Indications

Understanding more about how mindfulness is practiced illustrates the ways in which it can be effectively incorporated into counseling. Because of the aforementioned "monkey mind" with which people often struggle, meditation practice begins with focusing attention solely on the breath to gain some level of basic concentration. The most common practice involves a seated position. Though the cross-legged pose is common, it is most important that the meditator assume a posture that feels stable and promotes physical immobility and sustainability for an initial period of 20–30 minutes. The most essential element of the sitting posture is that one's back should be straight yet relaxed. Sustaining this posture may involve use of a chair or a wall for support. It is difficult, initially, to focus on the breath when one's hips, knees, or ankles may be aching! Although any of a number of hand postures (*mudras*) may be used, a common recommended pose is to place one hand in the other, palms facing up, with the hands just below the navel and the bend of each wrist pressed gently against the thigh. Most commonly, the eyes are closed throughout the meditation.

For beginning meditators, it is very common for the mind to wander. When this process happens, the meditator simply brings awareness back to the breath with gentle firmness. It is important to return to the breath without anger or judgment. When distractions become difficult to overcome, Gunaratana (2002) recommended either counting the breaths or focusing awareness on the point at the rim of the nostrils where the breath touches to enhance the concentration. Also, mindfulness often can be re-established with a few quick breaths. Initially, the duration of the meditation should be fairly brief—20–30 minutes— with the time predetermined. Setting an alarm can help the meditator focus without being distracted by issues of time. With sustained, successful practice, it will be natural to extend this time if one wishes to do so. Beginning meditators should generally meditate only one time each day to avoid overdoing it. Early in the morning and in the evening are good times to meditate. In the morning, a meditator is advised to first wash the face, shower, or lightly exercise to get circulation flowing. Counselors who have become better adept at incorporating mindfulness into their own lives may be ready to teach clients how to incorporate it into theirs. The mindfulness script at the end of the chapter provides an example of how to lead someone in a mindfulness meditation.

Cautions and Contraindications

When deciding to incorporate mindfulness practices in counseling, it is important to know the client, including his or her psychological status, counseling goals, and level of comfort with such a practice. Some clients may be uncomfortable with mindfulness, based on their religious and/or spiritual beliefs (Greason, 2011). There has been some question around using mindfulness with clients with psychosis, but researchers have shown that it may be beneficial (Jacobsen, Morris, Johns, & Hodkinson, 2011). Once again, it is chiefly important to consider the unique situation of each client when deciding whether or not to use mindfulness practices. If incorporating mindfulness would be beneficial, the following script can serve to guide the process.

Mindfulness Script

This brief mindfulness script focuses on breathing and may be used verbatim with a client. Before beginning the practice, it is helpful to invite client to assume a comfortable position, sitting upright, with feet planted firmly on the ground. From there, the client can be invited either to gently close the eyes or to softly gaze off the tip of the nose.

As you begin to settle into the moment, begin to notice the sensations in your body. Notice yourself softly settling deeper into your seat . . . almost as if all of the molecules in your body are settling like snowflakes in a snow globe. From there, gently draw your attention to your breathing—to the soft inhalation and exhalation of each breath. Begin to notice the beginnings and endings of each breath. Bring your awareness to where the breath originates from, how it softly flows into the body and gracefully moves into exhalation. Notice the quiet spaces between each inhalation and exhalation—those brief suspended moments in time. If your mind wanders, simply bring your attention back to the breath, without judgment.

Become curious about the depth of your breath. Where does it reach inside your body? Can you feel it in your nostrils, in the back of your throat, into your lungs, and perhaps, even down into your belly? Invite your breath to deepen, allowing it to expand your diaphragm and reach into your belly. If it helps you focus, gently place a hand on your stomach and feel the texture of your breath rising and falling, gracefully moving your hand up and down. Once again, if you notice your mind wandering, invite it to return back to the sensation of the breath, without judgment.

As you continue focusing, allow the gentle rising and falling of your breath to lead you deeper and deeper into a state of relaxation. Notice how each breath allows you to melt into the pure essence of this moment. Take some time to gently befriend your breath for a while. (Pause here for a lengthy period of time to allow participants space to practice mindfulness in silence.)

Very tenderly, allow yourself a moment of gratitude for your breath. Then, gently, begin to bring yourself back into the room. Notice where you are, the sounds around you, and the feel of your feet firmly planted on the ground. Then, whenever you feel ready, you can gently open up your eyes.

It is commonly said that mindfulness, while simple, is not easy. Over time, the development of deep concentration has the benefit of slowing down the thinking process and speeding up the awareness of this process (Gunaratana, 2002). With this development comes the ability to be aware of a thought without the ego-mind latching compulsively on to the thought. As mindfulness develops:

> . . . . you see yourself exactly as you are. You see your own foolish behavior. You see your own suffering . . . you see how you create that suffering. You see how you hurt others. You pierce right through the layer of lies that you normally tell yourself, and you see what is really there. Mindfulness leads to wisdom. (Gunaratana, 2002, pp. 152–153)

We invite you to enter into the great awareness of mindfulness, to see yourself as you are, and to cultivate greater wisdom—not only for yourself but also for the clients whom you guide and counsel along the way.

Suggested Resources

Online

Be Mindful [website]. http://bemindful.co.uk/
The Center for Mindfulness [website]. http://centerformindfulnessfresno
  .blogspot.com/

The Centre for Mindfulness Studies [website]. http://www
.mindfulnessstudies.com/
Just One Thing, by Rick Hanson, PhD [website]. http://www.rickhanson.net/
writings/just-one-thing
Mindfulnet [website]. http://mindfulnet.org/
UCLA Mindful Awareness Research Center [website]. http://marc.ucla.edu/
UMASS Center for Mindfulness [website]. http://www.umassmed.edu/cfm/
stress/index.aspx

References

Baer, R. A. (Ed.). (2010). *Assessing mindfulness and acceptance processes in
clients: Illuminating the theory and practice of change.* Oakland, CA:
New Harbinger.
Greason, P. (2011). Mindfulness. In C. S. Cashwell & J. S. Young (Eds.),
*Integrating spirituality and religion into counseling: A guide to competent
practice* (2nd ed.; pp. 183–208). Alexandria, VA: American Counseling
Association.
Gunaratana, B. H. (2002). *Mindfulness in plain English.* Boston, MA:
Wisdom.
Hanh, T. N. (1976). *The miracle of mindfulness: A manual on meditation.*
Boston, MA: Beacon Press.
Hanh, T. N. (1987). *Being peace.* Berkeley, CA: Parallax Press.
Hayes, S. C., Strosahl, K. D., & Wilson, K. G. (1999). *Acceptance and
commitment therapy: An experiential approach to behavior change.*
New York, NY: Guilford Press.
Jacobsen, P., Morris, E., Johns, L., & Hodkinson, K. (2011). Mindfulness
groups for psychosis: Key issues for implementation on an inpatient
unit. *Behavioural and Cognitive Psychotherapy, 39,* 349–353. doi:10.1017/
S1352465810000639
Kabat-Zinn, J. (1982). An outpatient program in behavioral medicine for
chronic pain patients based on the practice of mindfulness meditation:
Theoretical considerations and preliminary results. *General Hospital
Psychiatry, 4,* 33–47.
Kabat-Zinn, J. (1994). *Wherever you go, there you are: Mindfulness
meditation in everyday life.* New York, NY: Hyperion.
L'Amour, L. (n.d.). QuoteIdea [website]. Retrieved from http://www
.quoteidea.com/authors/louis-lamour-quotes

Linehan, M. M. (1993). *Cognitive-behavioral treatment of borderline personality disorder*. New York, NY: Guilford Press.

Parnell, C. (2002). *Meditation: A beginner's guide*. New York, NY: Barnes and Noble.

Segal, Z. V., Williams, J. M. G., & Teasdale, J. D. (2002). *Mindfulness-based cognitive therapy for depression*. New York, NY: Guilford Press.

Welwood, J. (2000). *Toward a psychology of being: Buddhism, psychotherapy, and the path of personal and spiritual transformation*. Boston, MA: Shambhala.

The Native American Medicine Sweat

Michael Tlanusta Garrett
Cyrus Williams
Mark Parrish
J. T. Garrett
Dale Brotherton

The Medicine Sweat is a Native American spiritual practice involved in the sweat lodge ceremony that honors the process of transformation and healing central to the modern-day practice of Native traditionalism across Native American nations. Many Native American traditionalists believe that in order to ensure harmony, balance, and wellness, one must participate in the ritualized cleansing of the mind, body, and spirit provided through the sweat lodge ceremony (Garrett & Garrett, 1996; 2002). This is a time for purifying oneself by joining with the powers of Mother Earth and those of the Universal Circle to give thanks and ask that oneself and others be blessed (Brown, 1972). As such, the Medicine Sweat is a widely accepted and practiced tradition that serves to purify those undergoing any sort of transformation, healing, or preparation.

In contrast to a popular Western perspective on individualized transformation as a fairly solitary process of self-actualization, traditional Native peoples have always believed that healing and transformation should take place in the presence of a person's support network, such as one's family, clan, and community, as a way of drawing on the natural support and understanding that exists within these relationships (Garrett, 1998; Garrett & Carroll, 2000). In this way, the sweat lodge ceremony serves a very sacred purpose through the ritual healing or cleansing of body, mind, and spirit, while bringing people together to honor the energy of life. Each person enters the lodge with individual concerns, and together, participants seek both individual and group

harmony and balance by sweating, praying, singing, talking, and sometimes just sitting together in silence.

Theoretical Foundation and Relevant Research

Increasingly, culturally based interventions and techniques such as
the sweat lodge ceremony or sweat therapy, based on Native traditions
of healing, are being used in clinical, mental health, correctional, and
substance abuse treatment centers serving both Native and non-Native
clients (Cohen, 2003; Smith, 2005; Thomason, 2000). Sweat therapy is
the combination of intense heat exposure with psychotherapy or counseling, ideally incorporating group process (Colmant, 2006). Though
little empirical evidence exists demonstrating the effectiveness of
sweat lodge ceremony or sweat therapy, because of its widespread and
increasing use across settings, it is important to better understand the
origin and current use of this culturally based intervention with Native
and non-Native populations.

A few studies indicate the significant impact of sweat lodge practice
on participants, both Native and non-Native (Colmant, 2006; Colmant,
Eason, Winterowd, Jacobs, & Cashel, 2005; Colmant & Merta, 1999,
2000; Garrett, Brubaker, Torres-Rivera, West-Olatunji, & Conwill,
2008; Gossage, Barton, Foster, Etsitty, Lone Tree, Leonard, & May, 2003;
Schiff & Moore, 2006). However, several researchers have examined
the physiological effects of sweating, and a few have examined, in particular, the benefits of sweat therapy. Benefits included enhancement
of neurological, respiratory, immune, and other human physiological
systems (Colmant et al., 2005; Dunn, 2004; Hannuksela & Ellahham,
2001; Smith, 2005). Sweat lodge therapy combines the physical benefits
of sweating with other therapeutic benefits that are realized in other
contemporary counseling approaches that together help clients more
than by relying on these approaches separately (Koss-Chioino, 2008).

The application of some form of Native American sweat in therapeutic settings has increased over the past few decades. In many instances,
use of the Native American sweat lodge in therapeutic settings has centered on attempts to offer culturally responsive services to Native clients
in a way that is congruent with their cultural way of life. In this vein,
application of traditions such as the sweat lodge ceremony has been
used with many Native and non-Native clients as a way to approach a
mending of the "broken Circle," an indigenous concept indicating the

potential neglect of traditional ways that can result in "dis-ease" or dis-harmony within the individual, family, clan, or community (Garrett & Carroll, 2000; Vick, Smith, & Iron Rope Herrera, 1998). This has been a central concept, for example, in the application of such traditional Native ceremonies in the treatment of alcoholism and other substance dependence issues at such facilities as residential treatment centers both on and off reservations (Thomason, 2000). Sweat lodges and other traditional healing approaches are also used in prisons as well as medical settings such as hospitals and clinics (Smith, 2005). In fact, more than 50% of the Indian Health Service (IHS) facilities currently make use of sweat lodges as complementary treatment (Cohen, 2003). It is important to reemphasize that this type of culturally responsive intervention, while unique, is not something new in terms of both historical ceremonial use and contemporary therapeutic intervention. A number of studies have shown the effectiveness of mental health counselors, therapists, and spiritual healers joining forces to work with individuals, groups, and communities (Gilene, Fish, & Draguns, 2004; Torres Rivera, 2005).

Definition/Description and History

Within Native nations, the use of varying forms of the sweat lodge or "hothouse" has been well documented, although the structure and process differ greatly from nation to nation (Oswalt, 2005). The importance of the sweat lodge ceremony among Native peoples has traditionally served many purposes including basic bathing; warmth; socialization as a form of schooling for the young to be taught their history, heritage, language, culture, myths, and religion; celebration; ceremonial cleansing; physical doctoring; spiritual training; and preparation for war, hunting, trips, marriage, vision quest, and various other rites of passage, cleansing, and healing (Colmant & Merta, 1999; Oswalt, 2005; Smith, 2005).

How the Sweat Lodge Came to Be

The following is an origin story shared by Robert Lake-Thom (Lake, 1991, pp. 153–154) of Karuk and Seneca descent, describing how the first sweat lodge came into existence and how it became a sacred healing tool for all peoples.

In the beginning, a long, long time ago, a sickness came to the First People. It was decided that a council should be held to discuss the problem. From every direction, all living beings came together in a great council to discuss the situation. For four days, they fasted, prayed, meditated, and sought visions and guidance together, seeking Medicine to help in some way.

Eagle and Hummingbird were the first to come into the Circle from east, bringing a spark from the Sun to light the sacred fire. Trees and Beaver were next to come in from the south, offering some wood for the fire, rocks from the Earth to surround it, and bringing their little sister, Tobacco, to make offerings. Bear came next from the west, bringing a basket filled with water from the rushing river to help contain the fire. From the north, Hawk and Deer came into the Circle bringing the quietness of wind to give breath of life to the sacred fire.

As the many clans of living beings talked and prayed together, no one noticed that the fire had become quite large. In a panic, Raven hustled over to the edge of the fire trying to help contain it, but as he got close, the fire singed his feathers black. Startled, he tripped over some of the rocks trying to get away from the heat, and knocked over Bear's basket full of water onto the fire. As it began to steam, Raven started squawking for help. Bear urged all the animals to hurry and cover Raven with their hides. As all the animals covered Raven, he continued to sing and began to sweat. In this way, the entire community had offered their support to Raven in his time of need.

When it was all over, Raven exclaimed that he had a great vision that this was to be called a Sweat Lodge that would be used for prayer and for healing. That is how the first Sweat Lodge came to be, and that is how Raven became known as a great doctor. But he never was a good singer. And so, it is good.

From this ancient story, one may connect to the seamless bond between nature, healing, and humankind, together represented in the cultural symbolism of the sweat lodge.

Elements of Native American Spirituality

Native American spirituality involved in the sweat lodge ceremony revolves around the essential concept of seeking harmony and balance in humans' relationship with the natural environment (Deloria, Silko, & Tinker, 2003). Balance in Native spirituality is a desired state wherein a person is in harmony with the universe—walking in step with the natural way (flow) of things, so to speak. Being in harmony means being in step with the universe and with its sacred rhythms, which is what many Native people refer to as "Good Medicine" (Garrett & Garrett, 2002; Garrett & Wilbur, 1999). By contrast, being in disharmony or "disease" means being out of step with the universe and its sacred rhythms, thereby inviting illness. Disharmony results when we humans are out of balance, our energies are unfocused or poorly focused, and we lose sight of our place in the universe. Overall wellness of the mind, body, spirit, and natural environment are an expression of the proper balance in the relationship of all things. If a person disturbs or disrupts the natural balance of relationship, illness or disease must be corrected through ceremony. This is one of the primary reasons for keeping personal life energy strong and clear in relation to others and to the natural environment.

For many Native Americans, the concept of health and wellness is not only a physical state but also a spiritual one. Therefore, within a cultural perspective that holds the land and community in the highest esteem, certain places in the natural environment are remembered within Native communities as sacred places where ceremonies are held to honor that sacred energy of life (Deloria et al., 2003; Garrett & Garrett, 2002; Hirschfelder & de Montano, 1998). These are the places where sweat lodges are constructed because, for traditional Native peoples, the place itself holds great spiritual power and significance in which to have healing take place in a proper way.

Cultural Symbolism of the Sweat Lodge

Though varying from nation to nation, the many elements comprising the sweat lodge ceremony hold deep cultural and spiritual significance. For instance, the very circular (sometimes oval) nature of the lodge itself represents both the Universe and the womb from which all life originates, with the stone pit at the center representing the all-encompassing power of the Creator in connection with the sacred fire in which the stones are heated. The stones used in the ceremony are symbolic of the unwavering, healing power of the Earth. Although different woods can be used for the poles that make up the structure, the most common of these is willow, which represents all growing things and the process of death and rebirth that creates the cycle of life. The willow (or other wood) saplings are set up to create four quadrants that represent the four cardinal directions of the Universe, also symbolizing the power of the four elements of fire, Earth, water, and wind. The water used in the ceremony not only is the one element essential to all living things, but also symbolizes the life-giving power of the Creator, and the steam that flows from being poured upon the hot stones represents the visible prayers of the people rising to the Creator, as well as the release of ancient knowledge contained within the stones, who are viewed as elders. The herbs and tobacco used in the ceremony also represent the energy of all living things through the sacredness of prayers being offered in a respectful manner (Garrett & Garrett, 2002).

Originally, many sweat lodges were covered with animal skins; in many instances today, blankets or tarps are used instead. The opening of the lodge is usually low, so that participants must get down on hands and knees to enter, symbolic of returning to the womb of Mother Earth in a humble manner, being immersed in total darkness once inside. By contrast, opening of the flap that covers the entrance to the lodge once inside represents liberation from the darkness of ignorance and ego in order to enter again into the world of truth, light, and goodness as a rebirth of spirit (Brown, 1972).

Indications and Cautions/Contraindications

Prominent use of the sweat lodge is already occurring in conjunction with counseling and various forms of therapeutic treatment. Indeed, sweat therapy is consistent with the greater attention to multicultural interventions in mental health counseling and the general appeal of alternative and complementary medicine (Kronenberg, Cushman, Wade, Kalmuss, & Chao, 2007). Although the sweat lodge is an appropriate fit for these trends, its integration into counseling practices, both for Native and non-Native clients, calls for attention to several factors, including who should participate, where the ceremony should be conducted, and who should conduct it.

Purpose and Logistics

Respect is essential, as the sweat lodge ceremony is sacred to Native peoples and should always be approached as such (Colmant & Merta, 1999). In addition to the earlier noted benefits, Smith (2005) pointed out that traditional healing methods like the sweat lodge ceremony may help Native clients explore and reconcile issues around cultural identity. In this pursuit, counselors may choose to refer individual clients to local sweats or to incorporate the sweat lodge in a group setting and should therefore consider ceremony logistics.

Medicine sweats can last anywhere from minutes to days, depending on the tribal tradition, the person conducting the ceremony, and the purpose of the sweat, as well as the needs of the persons involved in the ceremony. A serious misuse of the ceremony comes when it is approached by any of the participants as a test of endurance to prove one's power or strength. The sweat lodge ceremony is intended to serve just the opposite purpose: enabling participants to free themselves from pursuits that are driven by ego and the need for attention or power that can interfere with harmony and balance. More importantly, from a physical standpoint, to approach the ceremony as an endurance test can be dangerous, as it is physically taxing and can quickly take participants beyond their perceived physical limits. A good principle regarding this entire issue is to prefer quality rather than quantity. Participants are encouraged to drink plenty of water on the day of the sweat, eat lightly, and wear loose, comfortable, lightweight clothing.

Participants

From a purely physical standpoint, there are clear cautions against participation by people who would be adversely affected, such as pregnant women, people with heart conditions, or anyone taking medication who may be endangered from the physical strain of a prolonged sweat. Persons who are very underweight or overweight or those having difficulty regulating body temperature should also take caution. Furthermore, people who suffer from any condition such as claustrophobia or post-traumatic stress disorder are encouraged to avoid such a ceremony that might trigger uncomfortable reactions by being in a dark, closed space for an extended period of time.

A client will be chosen or referred to participate in the sweat lodge ceremony or sweat therapy based on desire for a more cultural or spiritual approach to gain balance in one's life; a desire to cleanse the mind, body, and spirit; or simply a belief that sweat lodge therapy would improve health when used in combination with conventional talk therapy. It is not unusual to find people who use complementary and alternative approaches along with conventional ones rather than conventional approaches alone (McCabe, 2007).

From a traditional Native perspective, there is the additional consideration of whether to conduct "mixed sweats," with men and women together. In many tribal traditions, there are strict spiritual taboos against conducting mixed sweats. The solution to this dilemma in many instances is to conduct separate sweats with leaders or facilitators who are of the same gender; this process can provide a powerful benefit in and of itself, for various reasons.

Leader and Locale

Also, in the traditional way, the leader of a sweat is a Medicine person with specialized cultural and spiritual training in the use of the sweat and other healing methods, according to the traditions of his or her nation. This person is chosen for training in the Medicine way either because of family lineage and/or special abilities with spirits and healing revealed to an existing Medicine person through demonstrated activity, or through spirit messages.

A controversial issue arises over considerations for where to conduct the ceremony and who should conduct it. From the perspective of many Native people, the "borrowing" of Native American healing practices and ceremonies has been problematic (Matheson, 1996), a result of the historical exploitation of Native peoples and culture by mainstream America (Aldred, 2000; Hernandez-Avila, 1996; Irwin, 1996). More specifically, misunderstanding has developed when non-Native people have attempted to interpret or conduct Native ceremonies or spiritual practices without understanding the meaning of Native ceremonies and practices or without being qualified to do so—that is, trained as a Medicine person in that tribal tradition.

For counselors, the most ideal scenario would be to have a qualified Native person conduct the ceremony in a traditional way (Schiff & Moore, 2006). However, if such a person is not available, they should be careful in selecting a non-Native person to lead a variation of the sweat ceremony or should be trained themselves, respecting the origins of this sacred practice.

Allying with the Surrounding Community

In each of these cases, it is important for counselors to obtain direct experience, if possible. Such experience with the sweat lodge enables counselors to speak from a more informed perspective when it comes to processing client experiences with the ceremony. Essential aspects to counselors becoming more knowledgeable about the sweat lodge ceremony would include talking and working alongside local Native community members if possible, obtaining permission to refer clients as needed for participation in the ceremony, attending a sweat within a Native context if invited, obtaining general information about Native traditions and ceremonies, reviewing more of the literature specifically on sweat lodge practices, and gaining some knowledge of local indigenous healers who might serve as allies in the healing process for clients. By increasing their own knowledge and understanding of this ancient tradition and current-day practice, practitioners will be more likely to honor the various Native traditions from which the ceremony comes and will provide a richer experience in counseling for those who participate in the ceremony as part of their therapeutic process. And when working in an agency setting, the counselor serves even more as a liaison, sharing this information and introducing the sweat lodge leader to agency clinicians and staff so they may support these efforts. Integrating indigenous approaches into one's professional repertoire is dependent on the professional counselor's ability to become the connection between one's practice and the community (Torres Rivera, 2005).

Summary

The following prayer is an example of that used in a Medicine sweat or sweat lodge ceremony:

> Oh Great Creator, we come before you in a humble manner and ask for your help. We offer these herbs and pray. To the four sacred directions and powers of the Universe we pray: to the spirits of the air in the north, to the spirits of the fire in the east, to the spirits of the Earth in the south, and to the spirits of the water in the west. We pray and

give thanks to the Grandfather Sun, the Grandmother Moon, to the Mother Earth, and all our relations in Nature. We thank you for your power, energy, gifts, and resources, because without you, we would not be able to live and survive. We ask that you forgive us if we have ever harmed or hurt you. We pray, offer this tobacco and these herbs, and ask that you doctor us, heal us, purify us, and protect us. We pray for our elders, women, children, and fellow human beings. We ask for peace, harmony, and healing worldwide. (Lake, 1991, pp. 173–174)

By all accounts, participation in the Medicine sweat can provide a deeply moving and truly spiritual experience that some participants have reportedly found physically, mentally, and spiritually beneficial. As Colmant and Merta (1999) described, "the sweating process in the ceremony requires mental and physical fortitude, bringing with it a strong sense of accomplishment, thus providing an ideal vehicle for those who want to commit to change" (p. 69). The intent is to restore the common bond between the sacred and the secular practice to wholeness and harmony through the Medicine sweat or sweat therapy that is being used in medical, clinical, mental health, correctional, and substance abuse treatment centers serving both Native and non-Native clients.

References

Aldred, L. (2000). Plastic shamans and astroturf sun dances. *American Indian Quarterly, 3,* 329–353.

Brown, J. E. (1972). *The sacred pipe: Black Elk's account of the seven rites of the Oglala Sioux.* New York, NY: Penguin.

Cohen, K. (2003). *Honoring the medicine: The essential guide to Native American healing.* New York, NY: Ballantine Books.

Colmant, S. (2006). The effects of sweat therapy on group therapeutic factors and feeling states. *Dissertation Abstracts International Section A: Humanities and Social Sciences, 66*(12–A), 42–96.

Colmant, S. A., Eason, E. A., Winterowd, C. L., Jacobs, S. C., & Cashel, C. (2005). Investigating the effects of sweat therapy on group dynamics and affect. *Journal for Specialists in Group Work, 30,* 329–341.

Colmant, S. A., & Merta, R. J. (1999). Using the sweat lodge ceremony as group therapy for Navajo youth. *Journal for Specialists in Group Work, 24,* 55–73.

Colmant, S. A., & Merta, R. J. (2000). Sweat therapy. *Journal for Specialists in Group Work, 23,* 31–38.

Deloria, V., Jr., Silko, L. M., & Tinker, G. E. (2003). *God is red: A Native view of religion.* Golden, CO: Fulcrum.

Dunn, S. (2004). Rituals of healing. *Natural Health, 34,* 57–62.

Garrett, J. T., & Garrett, M. T. (1996). *Medicine of the Cherokee: The way of right relationship.* Santa Fe, NM: Bear.

Garrett, J. T., & Garrett, M. T. (2002). *The Cherokee full circle: A practical guide to ceremonies and traditions.* Rochester, VT: Bear.

Garrett, M. T. (1998). *Walking on the wind: Cherokee teachings for healing through harmony and balance.* Santa Fe, NM: Bear.

Garrett, M. T., Brubaker, M., Torres-Rivera, E., West-Olatunji, C., & Conwill, W. L. (2008). The medicine of coming to center: Use of the Native American centering technique Ayeli—to promote wellness and healing in group work. *Journal for Specialists in Group Work, 33,* 179–198.

Garrett, M. T., & Carroll, J. (2000). Mending the broken circle: Treatment and prevention of substance abuse among Native Americans. *Journal of Counseling and Development, 78,* 379–388.

Garrett, M. T., & Garrett, J. T. (2002). Ayeli: Centering technique based on Cherokee spiritual traditions. *Counseling and Values, 46,* 149–158.

Garrett, M. T., & Garrett, J. T. (2003). *Native American faith in America.* New York, NY: Facts on File.

Garrett, M. T., & Osborne, W. L. (1995). The Native American sweat lodge as metaphor for group work. *Journal for Specialists in Group Work, 20,* 33–39.

Garrett, M. T., & Wilbur, M. P. (1999). Does the worm live in the ground? Reflections on Native American spirituality. *Journal of Multicultural Counseling and Development, 27,* 193–206.

Gilene, U. P., Fish, J. M., & Draguns, J. G. (Eds). (2004). *Handbook of culture, therapy, and healing.* Mahwah, NJ: Lawrence Erlbaum.

Gossage, J. P., Barton, L., Foster, L., Etsitty, L., Lone Tree, C., Leonard, C., & May, P. A. (2003). Sweat lodge ceremonies for jail-based treatment. *Journal of Psychoactive Drugs, 35,* 33–42.

Hannuksela, M. L., & Ellahham, S. (2001). Benefits and risks of sauna bathing. *American Journal of Medicine, 110,* 118–126.

Hernandez-Avila, I. (1996). Meditations of the spirit: Native American religious traditions and the ethics of representation. *American Indian Quarterly, 20,* 329–353.

Hirschfelder, A., & de Montano, M. (1998). *The Native American almanac: A portrait of Native America today.* New York, NY: Macmillan.

Irwin, L. (1996). Themes in Native American spirituality. *American Indian Quarterly, 20,* 309–327.

Koss-Chioino, J. (2008, January). Review of complementary and alternative treatments in mental health care. *Journal of Nervous and Mental Disease, 196,* 86.

Kronenberg, F., Cushman, L. F., Wade, C. M., Kalmuss, D., & Chao, M. T. (2007). Race/ethnicity and women's use of complementary and alternative medicine in the United States: Results of a national survey. *American Journal of Public Health, 96,* 1236–1242.

Lake, M. G. (1991). *Native healer: Initiation into an ancient art.* Wheaton, IL: Quest Books.

Matheson, L. (1996). Valuing spirituality among Native American populations. *Counseling and Values, 41,* 51–58.

McCabe, G. H. (2007). The healing path: A culture and community-derived Indigenous therapy model. *Psychotherapy: Theory/Research/Practice, 44,* 148–160.

Oswalt, W. H. (2005). *This land was theirs: A study of Native North Americans* (8th ed.). New York, NY: McGraw-Hill.

Schiff, J. W., & Moore, K. (2006). The impact of the sweat lodge ceremony on dimensions of well-being. *American Indian and Alaska Native Mental Health Research: The Journal of the National Center, 13,* 48–69.

Smith, D. P. (2005). The sweat lodge as psychotherapy. In R. Moodley & W. West (Eds.), *Integrating traditional healing into counseling and psychotherapy* (pp. 196–209). Thousand Oaks, CA: Sage.

Thomason, T. C. (2000). Issues in the treatment of Native Americans with alcohol problems. *Journal of Multicultural Counseling and Development, 28,* 248–252.

Torres Rivera, E. (2005). Espiritismo: The flywheel of the Puerto Rican spiritual traditions. *Interamerican Journal of Psychology, 39*(2), 295–300.

Vick, R. D., Sr., Smith, L. M., & Iron Rope Herrera, C. (1998). The healing circle: An alternative path to alcoholism recovery. *Counseling and Values, 42,* 132–141.

Near-Death Experiences

Janice Miner Holden

Throughout history and across cultures, people have occasionally reported that during a life-threatening illness or injury that they had survived, they had had unique, unexpected psychological experiences that transformed them (Holden, Greyson, & James, 2009; Kellehear, 2009). Because of advances in resuscitation and other life-saving technology during the second half of the twentieth century, people were reporting these experiences in unprecedented numbers. In 1975, Raymond Moody, a psychiatrist and philosopher, wrote the now-classic book *Life After Life,* in which he coined the term "near-death experience" (NDE) and introduced the phenomenon to the public and to most professionals (Moody, 1975/2001). By 2005, researchers had conducted over 65 studies involving over 2,500 near-death experiencers (NDErs; Holden et al., 2009). In these studies, they addressed many questions about NDEs, including circumstances, contents, incidence, and aftereffects. Regarding incidence, approximately one in five survivors of a close brush with death reports an NDE (Zingrone & Alvarado, 2009), and it is estimated that 15 million people in the US alone have had an NDE (Taylor & van Lommel, 2006). Because NDErs are among the clientele of medical, psychological, social, and spiritual healthcare providers, these professionals have addressed the needs of NDErs and their associates and how best to be of help in the aftermaths of NDEs. The following material contains a summary of what is currently known and speculated on these topics.

NDE Contents

An NDE is a distinctive subjective experience with paranormal and mystical features that sometimes is reported after a near-death episode (Greyson, 2000). A near-death episode is the situation of clinical death, imminent death, or perceived imminent death that occurs in circumstances including illness, accident, and suicide attempt. Experiences indistinguishable from NDEs occur during other extreme circumstances, such as the extreme sadness of profound grief and the extreme relaxation and introspection of deep meditation. According to many NDErs, the term "near-death" is a misnomer; they are adamant that they were *in* death, not just *near* death.

Researchers have identified two basic types of NDEs, distinguishable by the predominant emotional tone of the experience: pleasurable or distressing (Greyson, 2000). Whereas pleasurable NDEs (pNDEs) are dominated by feelings of love, joy, peace, equanimity, and/or bliss (Zingrone & Alvarado, 2009), distressing NDEs (dNDEs) are dominated by feelings of confusion, resistance, horror, isolation, and/or guilt, usually resulting in terror (Bush, 2009). Of all people who report an NDE, the vast majority reports a pleasurable experience. Whether distressing experiences truly are infrequent or just infrequently reported is not known. In any case, most NDErs of both types report that the experience was as real as or more real than their usual waking experience of reality.

The prototypic pNDE includes three aspects that tend to occur in a particular order. However, NDEs actually vary by individual as to what aspect(s) occur, the order in which they occur, and the specific contents of a given aspect (Greyson, 2000).

In the *disassociated* aspect, the pNDEr reports having experienced a peaceful, floating sensation disassociated from identification with the body or with any definable perspective. In the *material* aspect, the person reports having perceived the physical, material world— typically one's body and the adjacent area but sometimes distant from one's body—from a perspective outside of the body. In this aspect, people often report normal plus paranormal perception, such as being able simultaneously to see, and to see through, walls. Some of the most compelling reports indicating the "reality" of the NDE are cases of *apparently non-physical veridical perception*—perception of specific, unique events that the person should not have been able to perceive, considering the physical body's condition and/or position, but that later is, nevertheless, corroborated as accurate (Holden, 2009). These cases include NDE vision in congenitally blind persons and vision and hearing in a woman who was monitored during deep anesthesia and whose eyes were taped shut and ears blocked (Rivas, Dirven, & Smit, 2016).

In the *transmaterial* aspect, the pNDEr perceives and interacts with environments and entities not of the physical, material world.

Perceptions may include seeing preternatural environments in which objects appeared lit from within; hearing celestial music; encountering deceased loved ones and/or other spiritual entities; communicating telepathically with those entities; moving rapidly through a tunnel or void toward a light; and entering the light, which the experiencer realized was actually an all-knowing, all-loving being. Typically, while in the light, the pNDEr may have experienced a panoramic life review in which the experiencer simultaneously re-viewed, re-experienced, and experienced being on the receiving end of one's actions throughout life; and, beyond the light, seeing "cities" of light and knowledge.

At some point, the pNDEr perceived having returned to the physical body (Greyson, 2000; Zingrone & Alvarado, 2009). About half of NDErs report they had a choice about whether or not to return; when they chose to return, it was in response to a love connection with one or more living people. The other half reported not remembering having made a choice: They either were told or made to return, or they were just suddenly "back" in their bodies. Some NDErs do not remember reentry into the physical body, whereas others recall reentering through any of a number of locations such as the head, the chest, or the entire body.

Distressing NDErs have reported four types of experience (Bush, 2009), which are listed here in order from most- to least-reported. In the *powerlessness* type, the features are the same as in a pNDE, but the experiencer feels powerless and, consequently, resistant, fearful, and/or angry. In the *nothingness* type, the dNDEr is acutely aware of nonexistence or of being completely alone in an absolute and eternal void. In the *torment* type, the dNDEr experiences ugly or foreboding landscapes, demonic beings, annoying noises, frightening creatures, and/or other human spirits in extreme distress. The fourth type is reported extremely rarely: Unlike the pNDE life review in which the experiencer feels only love and acceptance from the being of light, despite one's most unloving acts in life, in the *worthlessness* type of dNDE, the experiencer feels negatively judged by a Higher Power during the life review.

NDE Aftereffects

Aftereffects of both pleasurable and distressing NDEs are both short- and long-term, and, with one exception, are quite similar. The exception involves subsequent fear of death: Whereas virtually all pNDErs completely lose their fear of death, dNDErs sometimes evidence an increase in that fear—at least in the short term (Bush, 2009; Holden, 2013; Noyes, Fenwick, Holden, & Christian, 2009).

Short-term aftereffects are physical, such as pain and a sense of confinement in the body; emotional, such as anger, sadness, longing, or relief; social, either increased withdrawal or increased talkativeness as a result of preoccupation with the NDE; and usually spiritual, involving a sense that the experience was an entry into a spiritual domain (Noyes et al., 2009).

Long-term effects are numerous (Noyes et al., 2009). Psychologically, NDErs often experience grief over the loss of the experience of unconditional love in the NDE; an increased sense of self-acceptance, -confidence, and -worth; and stress over reconciling new beliefs and values with one's prior lifestyle. Value changes include less concern with materialism and fame as well as a greater sensitivity to and concern for others, reduced tolerance for violence, increased appreciation of life, and increased sense of purpose in life. Spiritually, NDErs often report a sense of ongoing connectedness to a "higher" domain/deity, an increase in paranormal experiences such as psychic and out-of-body experiences and healing ability, and an increased commitment either to independent spiritual pursuit or, less often, to organized religion. Physically, many NDErs report increased allergies, sensitivity to chemicals, and electromagnetic phenomena such as the inability to keep one's wristwatch operational or of malfunctioning of lights and/or computers in NDErs' vicinity (Nouri & Holden, 2008).

All these aftereffects are highly likely to result in social changes and stress (Noyes et al., 2009). Most NDErs say the experience was far-and-away the most profound of their lives. Because the NDE is ineffable—impossible to explain fully in human language—NDErs often have difficulty making the profundity of their experiences understood by others who may reject, discount, pathologize, or demonize the experience and/or experiencers. NDErs' changes in values undermine the implicit contracts upon which pre-NDE social relationships had been based—friendships, marriages, and employment. Indeed, many researchers have observed a high incidence of changes in social group, intimate partner (Christian & Holden, 2012), and occupation.

NDEr Demographics and Special Populations

No demographic variable—age, sex, education, religious affiliation or non-affiliation, socioeconomic class, sexual orientation, life history of "good" or "bad" deeds, level of mental health, type of near-death episode, etc.—predicts who will have an NDE or whether an NDE will be pleasurable or distressing (Holden, Long, & MacLurg, 2009). Some researchers have detected higher levels of a very few psychological traits, such as absorption—the ability to focus on an object of attention to the exclusion of extraneous stimuli. However, because these studies were retrospective, it cannot be known whether absorption facilitated the NDE or whether the NDE facilitated absorption. Cross-cultural studies have revealed certain universal components, such as a spiritual otherworld, spiritual entities (Kellehear, 2009), and encountering a border between the earthly and spiritual domains; one's culture and personal learning history appear to influence the exact form of those components and the experiencer's interpretation of them (Kellehear, 2009) but cannot fully explain them (Greyson, Kelly, & Kelly, 2009).

Of particular interest are children's and suicide attempters' NDEs. Young children's NDEs contain the same aspects as adults' NDEs but tend to be less complex than those of adults, apparently reflecting experiencers' cognitive and verbal development (Sutherland, 2009). Regarding suicide attempters, whereas in general a person who has attempted suicide is more prone to attempt again, adult suicide attempters who had an NDE appear to be substantially less prone to attempt again; they have learned that their lives have purpose, that life is a gift, and that challenging life circumstances are to be managed and overcome as opportunities to deepen one's capacity for love and increased knowledge (Greyson, 2000).

Indications and Contraindications

Because of NDE incidence, counselors are likely to have NDErs among their clientele. A report of an NDE and its aftereffects does not typically warrant a diagnosis of psychopathology, though some NDErs may meet the criterion for post-traumatic stress disorder (Foster, James, & Holden, 2009; Greyson, 2000). More typically, the appropriate diagnosis is the *DSM-5* V-code of Religious or Spiritual Problem (American Psychiatric Association, 2013). As in the normal population, some NDErs do exhibit coexisting psychopathology, which should be addressed as such (Greyson, 2000).

Perhaps the single most important counselor intervention is empathic listening. Research indicates that a listener's response of acceptance, understanding, and exploration of the unfolding meaning of the NDE for the experiencer tends to set the NDEr on a course of positive integration of the experience. Conversely, disbelief, discounting, and pathologizing tend to foster withdrawal and a delay—sometimes for years—of integration (Foster et al., 2009; Noyes et al., 2009).

Another potentially helpful intervention is including an NDEr's close associates—family members and friends—in the counseling process. Close associates' responses to the NDEr also are important for the NDEr's constructive integration of the experience, and those associates themselves may need support to the degree that the NDEr is "a different person" after the experience. In particular, associates' accepting, non-pathologizing response is important, as is their having realistic expectations of the NDEr, including not expecting the NDEr to become saintly (Foster et al., 2009; Greyson, 2000).

Both the NDEr and close associates can benefit greatly from psychoeducation (Foster et al., 2009). Information resulting from now-extensive research, and referral to resources such as quality readings, websites, and support groups—including, if available, one of the approximately 50 U.S. local Friends of the International Association for Near-Death Studies (IANDS) support and interest groups—can enhance understanding and provide an atmosphere facilitative of coping with the often upheaving aftermath of an NDE.

Use of visual and auditory expressive arts may be a particularly appropriate medium to help an NDEr express nonverbally—and then, perhaps, increasingly verbally—the ineffable aspects of the experience. Cognitive therapy is appropriate if the NDEr evidences distorted beliefs, such as a tendency toward "ego-inflation"—the belief that, having had an unusual experience, one is wholly unique, superior, and separate from others. Eyes-closed techniques, such as Focusing (Gendlin, 1982) and guided imagery, can be helpful in response to NDErs' often-reported aftereffect of a compelling sense that one is meant to accomplish some purpose in life, accompanied by a frustrating uncertainty as to exactly what that purpose is. Child-centered play therapy (Landreth, 2012) may be especially appropriate for NDErs aged 2–10. Overall, a counselor with a theoretical orientation that includes an explicitly transpersonal aspect, such as Roberto Assagioli's Psychosynthesis (see entry elsewhere in this volume), Ken Wilber's Integral Counseling (Fall, Holden, & Marquis, 2010), or Carl Jung's analytical psychology (Jung, 1989), may be particularly facilitative for an NDEr client.

No researchers have conducted studies on counseling in the aftermath of NDEs. In the absence of such research, the expression of the core conditions of counseling through the use of basic counseling skills and the use of systemic interventions, psychoeducation, referral to support resources, and specific change strategies geared to the particular needs of each NDEr client, are probably the most appropriate.

Suggested Resources

Print

Holden, J. M., Greyson, B., & James, D. (Eds.). (2009). *The handbook of near-death experiences: Thirty years of investigation.* Santa Barbara, CA: Praeger/ABC-CLIO.

Kason, Y. (2008). *Farther shores: Exploring how near-death, kundalini, and mystical experiences can transform ordinary lives.* Bloomington, IN: iUniverse.

Ring, K., & Valarino, E. E. (1998). *Lessons from the light: What we can learn from the near-death experience.* New York, NY: Insight/Plenum. Probably the single best book for NDErs and their close associates to understand the NDE and cope with its aftereffects.

Online

Holden, J. M. (2015). Responding to near-death experiencers and other potentially spiritually transformative experiences: Recommendations for healthcare providers. Available at http://www.coe.unt.edu/sites/default/files/22/129/14_NDE_Acronym_Handout.pdf

International Association for Near-Death Studies (IANDS): www.iands.org Contains a wealth of information and referral resources, including informational brochures, a recommended reading list, and a listing of locations of local Friends of IANDS support and interest groups, as well as video recordings from the organization's annual conferences.

Near-Death.com [website]: www.near-death.com

Near-Death Experience Research Foundation: www.nderf.org

References

American Psychiatric Association (2013). *Diagnostic and statistical manual of mental disorders* (5th ed.). Washington, DC: American Psychiatric Association.

Bush, N. E. (2009). Distressing Western near-death experiences: Finding a way through the abyss. In J. M. Holden, B. Greyson, & D. James (Eds.), *The handbook of near-death experiences: Thirty years of investigation* (pp. 63–86). Santa Barbara, CA: Praeger/ABC-CLIO.

Christian, R., & Holden, J. M. (2012). "'Til death do us part": Marital aftermath of one spouse's near-death experience. *Journal of Near-Death Studies, 30*(4), 207–231.

Fall, K., Holden, J. M., & Marquis, A. (2010). *Theoretical models of counseling and psychotherapy* (2nd ed.). New York, NY: Routledge.

Foster, R. D., James, D., & Holden, J. M. (2009). Practical applications of near-death experiences research. In J. M. Holden, B. Greyson, & D. James (Eds.), *The handbook of near-death experiences: Thirty years of investigation* (pp. 235–258). Santa Barbara, CA: Praeger/ABC-CLIO.

Gendlin, E. T. (1982). *Focusing* (2nd rev. ed.). New York, NY: Bantam Books.

Greyson, B. (2000). Near-death experiences. In E. Cardeña, S. J. Lynn, & S. Krippner (Eds.), *Varieties of anomalous experience: Examining the scientific evidence* (pp. 315–352). Washington, DC: American Psychological Association.

Greyson, B., Kelly, E. W., & Kelly, E. F. (2009). Explanatory models for near-death experiences. In J. M. Holden, B. Greyson, & D. James (Eds.), *The handbook of near-death experiences: Thirty years of investigation* (pp. 213–234). Santa Barbara, CA: Praeger/ABC-CLIO.

Holden, J. M. (2009). Veridical perception in near-death experiences. In J. M. Holden, B. Greyson, & D. James (Eds.), *The handbook of near-death experiences: Thirty years of investigation* (pp. 185–212). Santa Barbara, CA: Praeger/ABC-CLIO.

Holden, J. M. (2013). After-math: Counting the aftereffects of potentially spiritually transformative experiences. *Journal of Near-Death Studies, 31*(2), 65–78.

Holden, J. M., Greyson, B., & James, D. (2009). The field of near-death studies: Past, present, and future. In J. M. Holden, B. Greyson, & D. James (Eds.), *The handbook of near-death experiences: Thirty years of investigation* (pp. 1–16). Santa Barbara, CA: Praeger/ABC-CLIO.

Holden, J. M., Long, J., & MacLurg, B. J. (2009). Characteristics of near-death experiencers. In J. M. Holden, B. Greyson, & D. James (Eds.),

The handbook of near-death experiences: Thirty years of investigation (pp. 109–134). Santa Barbara, CA: Praeger/ABC-CLIO.

Jung, C. G. (1989). *Memories, dreams, reflections* (Rev. ed.). C. Winston & R. Winston (Trans.). A. Jaffe (Ed.). New York, NY: Random House (original publication 1963).

Kellehear, A. (2009). Census of non-Western near-death experiences in 2005: Observations and critical reflections. In J. M. Holden, B. Greyson, & D. James (Eds.), *The handbook of near-death experiences: Thirty years of investigation* (pp. 135–158). Santa Barbara, CA: Praeger/ABC-CLIO.

Landreth, G. L. (2012). *Play therapy: The art of the relationship* (3rd ed.). New York, NY: Routledge.

Moody, R. (2001). *Life after life: The investigation of a phenomenon—survival of bodily death.* San Francisco, CA: Harper. (Original work published 1975)

Nouri, F. M., & Holden, J. M. (2008). Electromagnetic aftereffects of near-death experiences. *Journal of Near-Death Studies, 27*(2), 83–110.

Noyes, R., Fenwick, P., Holden, J. M., & Christian, R. (2009). Aftereffects of pleasurable Western adult near-death experiences. In J. M. Holden, B. Greyson, & D. James (Eds.), *The handbook of near-death experiences: Thirty years of investigation* (pp. 41–62). Santa Barbara, CA: Praeger/ABC-CLIO.

Rivas, T., Dirven, A., & Smit, R. H. (2016). *The self does not die: Verified paranormal phenomena from near-death experiences.* Durham, NC: International Association for Near-Death Studies.

Sutherland, C. (2009). "Trailing clouds of glory": The near-death experiences of Western children and teens. In J. M. Holden, B. Greyson, & D. James (Eds.), *The handbook of near-death experiences: Thirty years of investigation* (pp. 87–108). Santa Barbara, CA: Praeger/ABC-CLIO.

Taylor, S., & van Lommel, P. (2006). *Pleasurable Western adult near-death experiences: Circumstances, contents, and incidence.* (Videorecording available at http://www.iands.org/conferences/2006_conference _presentations/)

Zingrone, N. L., & Alvarado, C. S. (2009). Pleasurable Western adult near-death experiences: Features, circumstances, and incidence. In J. M. Holden, B. Greyson, & D. James (Eds.), *The handbook of near-death experiences: Thirty years of investigation* (pp. 17–40). Santa Barbara, CA: Praeger/ABC-CLIO.

Past-Life Therapy

Janice Miner Holden

Spontaneous memories of previous lives have been the experience of people throughout history and across cultures (Stevenson, 2001, pp. 29–40). University of Virginia psychiatrist Ian Stevenson (1974, 1997, 2001, 2003) is probably best known for his research on people who remember previous lives. Nearly four decades of research on primarily Western near-death experiences reveals that they often include past-life memories (Zingrone & Alvarado, 2009), resulting in experiencers becoming more open to the concept of reincarnation (Noyes, Fenwick, Holden, & Christian, 2009). Clients have sometimes spontaneously reported experiences of past-life memories during altered state work in psychotherapy—often to the great dismay of therapists for whom the concept of past lives is entirely foreign and who therefore feel completely unprepared to respond (Weiss, 1988). For these and other reasons, psychotherapists have been pondering for decades whether facilitating past-life memories in clients might be therapeutically beneficial to them—in some cases, citing clinical experience to support their adamant assertion that it indeed is.

Some time just prior to 1996, I attended a 3-hour presentation on past-life regression by psychologist Roger Woolger. Then, in the summer of 1996 in upstate New York, I attended two back-to-back, week-long professional trainings on past-life therapy: one led by psychiatrist Brian Weiss and the other led by a group from California, the Professional Institute for Regression Training, that included psychologists Winafred Lucas and Ronald Jue. With this experiential background, I undertook an investigation into past-life therapy literature, a summary of which I present in this chapter. I illustrate several of the points from one of my own past-life therapy experiences.

In 1993, Lucas published a two-volume work entitled *Regression Therapy: A Handbook for Professionals*. A hallmark of this work is that it contains submissions by several highly experienced past-life therapists, all answering the same questions Lucas had posed regarding their theoretical and technical approaches, as well as Lucas's integrated summary of their points. Although other authors have since published summaries of past-life therapy, such as Jue (1996), and many authors have published their own approaches (for example, Moody, 1990; Weiss, 1993, 2012; Woolger, 1988, 2004), Lucas's work remains classic for its integrated summary of several past-life therapists' clinical perspectives and practices, revealing the deep structure of the approach and how it manifests in the surface structure of each therapist's unique method.

Past-life therapy rests historically on the foundation of Sigmund Freud's use of regression in psychoanalysis and Carl Jung's use of active imagination in analytical psychology (Lucas, 1993). Therapists can lead groups in past-life regression (Wambach, 1993), but they more typically conduct it with individual clients. The practice begins with both client and counselor at least being open to, if not believing in, the potential that facilitating and processing clients' memories of seemingly previous lifetimes can promote their healing and development. Some therapists and/or clients believe in reincarnation, and others do not; such belief is not necessary for clients to benefit from the therapy.

The Process

Prior to beginning the process, past-life therapists carry out standard legal and clinical psychotherapy practices, such as procuring the client's informed consent and taking a thorough client history. Past-life therapy is appropriate for clients with good ego functioning and either a physical or psychological symptom or an existential question that traditional methods have not resolved or completely resolved. It is contraindicated for clients too skeptical to consider the practice potentially helpful even as only a metaphor, those for whom the practice in some way violates their personal and/or spiritual/religious belief system, those extremely low in introspection, those in crisis, and those seeking to use the technique for sensationalism or to avoid the challenges of everyday life and personal development. Most therapists consider the approach contraindicated for clients with psychotic or borderline personality disorder and for children (Lucas, 1993).

Preparation for past-life therapy is indicated if a client has not previously done introspective experiential work in psychotherapy. As it typically is conducted with the client's eyes closed, the therapist needs to confirm that the client has no objection to such work; in the relatively rare case when closed eyes are contraindicated, the therapist can suggest an alternative such as fixing the eyes, defocused, on a benign spot in the room. The therapist can explain that past-life memories usually are visual but sometimes involve the other senses such as hearing, feeling, and/or smelling and tasting. To help the client get a sense of the process of having the inner experience of the past-life memory while simultaneously remaining in contact with the therapist, the client can be invited to close his or her eyes (or fix the gaze), to imagine being at home, and to talk the therapist through the beginning minute or two of a tour of the home, starting at the front door—with the therapist occasionally asking a question to which the client responds. Thus the client experiences how phenomena may unfold in the mind's eye while he or she remains in interactive communication with the therapist. The therapist also should forewarn the client that past-life memories sometimes evoke strong emotion and should, in the unlikely but possible case the memory becomes too distressing, agree with the client on some temporary distancing strategies—such as assuming a disembodied "observer" position to the scene or going to a psychological safe place—or permanent discontinuation strategies such as opening one's eyes and focusing on the room and the therapist. The client can be encouraged to remember that anything seen in the mind's eye is not actually currently happening and, thus, does not represent a real threat to one's actual present wellbeing.

Once a client is deemed a good candidate for past-life therapy and has been oriented to the approach, therapist and client identify a *bridge* to past-life memory. The bridge is, in essence, the issue the client wishes to resolve. It may be a chronic physical sensation or condition, an enigmatic psychosocial concern—such as a persistent troubling emotion, behavior pattern, or feeling toward another person that has no apparent source—or a persistent existential question. In one of my experiences, I focused on the chronic intermittent pain I had experienced in my right hip for the previous few years; it had been diagnosed medically as benign joint pain, but it was painful enough that when it flared up, I would use analgesic medication, which was uncharacteristic of me.

Having settled on the bridge, the therapist uses some *induction technique*. The client is instructed to get comfortable by loosening any tight garment and lying down on a mat or reclining in a recliner chair. The client then holds the bridge in the back of one's mind while listening to and following the therapist's voice. I have experienced two forms of induction: hypnosis and progressive relaxation, both involving guided imagery such as going down a staircase through a door, age regression, or rising up into a condition beyond space and time and then returning to earth at another space and time from the past. I have found all approaches equally successful, and some therapists use yet other approaches (Jue, 1996; Lucas, 1993); therapists seem to use whatever technique they were schooled in and resonate most with. The client is instructed to remain open and attentive to any image that may emerge from any sensory modality and then to stay with that image and allow it to expand. In the beginning of my experience, I saw white cloth as if through a microscope and felt the emotion of profound relief; as I stayed with the image, it expanded, revealing a bandage around my splinted right leg; my left leg was in a gray pantleg; I was a Civil War soldier named Roy, sitting under a tree on a beautiful spring day; I had fallen from my horse during battle and suffered a severe but clean break; my relief was that the surgeon—rather than amputating as was the common practice—had set and splinted my leg, believing it would heal in time, and I was waiting to go home, my service completed.

The client typically feels personally identified with one character in the story—that the character is "me"—and the story usually takes on a life of its own, almost always with contents quite surprising and unexpected to the client and almost always involving a mundane rather than well-known historical figure. The therapist then employs several strategies to facilitate a *deepening* of the experience: helping clients experience themselves fully in the story (Lucas, 1993). In addition to basic reflective counseling skills and open-ended questions, therapists might ask rather standard specific questions such as, "Look down at your feet; what do you see?" From this observation, the client may be able to determine race, age, gender, and/or culture in the imaged story. The therapist will typically encourage the client to use present tense in describing what he or she is experiencing ("I arrive home safely and keep my leg splinted for three months. Now the splint has been removed, and my leg is permanently frozen in a straight position, such that I have to walk like Chester in the TV show *Gunsmoke*. This puts a terrible strain on my right hip. My fiancé, Nancy, with whom I'd had a pact that we would marry if I returned from battle, now sees me as disabled and will not marry me."). The therapist typically encourages the client to feel the physical and emotional sensations of the lifetime. ("I do leather work and partner with the town blacksmith to create horse paraphernalia. Every night I go home to my one-room cabin and live alone and feel profoundly lonely. I develop a deep and abiding sense of bitterness and anger.") The therapist develops techniques to help the client move backward and forward in the lifetime as needed, such as, "In a moment, I'll count to three, and you'll move to the next significant event in this lifetime. One, two, three." Ultimately, the client typically moves to and through the death in that lifetime and then takes a detached observational stance to consider what in that lifetime might inform a healthier current lifetime—which opens the door to the *processing* phase.

In my case, as I lay on the mat pondering that latter point, I found that even in death, I could not free myself from a pervasive sense of profound bitterness and anger—very uncharacteristic of how I experience myself in this lifetime. My therapist suggested I bring in a spirit guide to help me get another, potentially more helpful perspective, which I did. At one point, my therapist said something of which I have no memory (and would give a lot of money right now to know!), and, my eyes still closed, I burst into tears, sat up, and for a few minutes wept profusely, eyes still closed, rocking back and forth, rubbing my leg, saying over and over again, "This poor leg! This poor leg!" Eventually I felt emotionally finished, stopped crying, and opened my eyes—and felt the profound relief of completed abreaction. Though the following words were not part of that experience, they describe my inner process: My leg and I had been victims of the Civil War—of man's inhumanity to man; it was as if my right hip held all the anguish of the physical and psychological pain—the rejection and profound loneliness—that had been the fruits of that inhumanity. In my tears, my bitterness and anger that had been "stuck" in that form turned to an all-encompassing sadness and grief that I could express and release.

Because this experience occurred during one of the training weeks, I did not have the opportunity for follow-up processing that would be possible in ongoing therapy. Such processing is typical, in which therapist and client can expand on results and lessons learned from the past-life experience. Sometimes clients remember multiple lifetimes involving a similar theme that is salient and relevant to the client's current life, which can deepen the clarity of the theme.

Following my experience, I "watched" with interest as first days, then weeks, then months passed without a return of pain to my hip. In the years that followed, I had recurrent hip pain on three occasions—the last on the occasion of 9/11. In each case, upon detecting the pain,

I stopped and introspected whether I might be holding anger toward someone for inhumane action, and in every case, I quickly identified the source of the emotional/physical pain and, through one process or another, released it—after which the pain quickly dissolved. In my case, I am grateful to have been able to forego considerable pain and medication, apparently as a result of that past-life session.

Concluding Remarks and Considerations

Weiss (1996) has indicated that even he, to whom patients come specifically to experience past-life therapy, finds the need to use the technique in only about 40% of cases; in most cases, resolution of the issue for which the patient seeks relief is achieved with reference to experiences from this lifetime (p. 5). Lucas (1993) warned therapists that even when past-life therapy seems indicated, they should maintain realistic expectations. Some clients will have a past-life memory on the first attempt, but others will need to try the technique several times before experiencing imagery, and a few will never "succeed" in experiencing a past life. Of those who do, some may experience immediate transformation, but more typically the fruits of the experience will ripen over time as therapist and client revisit the experience and its associated themes throughout the course of therapy.

During the two residential training weeks, I lived among two groups of therapists-in-training and observed that two topics dominated the discussions of both groups. One topic was amazement at the availability of these stories within our psyches. Through demonstrations and practices, just by lying down, relaxing, and going through a relatively brief induction, one surprising story after another would bubble up into consciousness—often complete with great detail about the living conditions and subjective experiences of a lifetime in another time and place. We were astonished at the accessibility of these often full-blown stories, as if they resided just below the surface of our consciousness, simply waiting to be invited forth. The other topic was the question of the reality of the experiences. On the one hand, they *felt* absolutely real; on the other, our rational minds asked how they *could* possibly be! Those discussions usually ended in the only partially satisfying conclusion that whether or not they were real memories of past lives, they almost always had psychological relevance—sometimes highly impactful—for living more healthfully and fulfillingly in this lifetime.

In this way, our experience during those trainings—and my subsequent experience using past-life therapy in my counseling practice—coincided with the clinical reports of past-life therapists who have asserted the unique benefits of the approach.

That being said, past-life therapy remains an essentially unresearched therapeutic modality. In a search of publications listed in PsycINFO since Lucas's and Jue's summaries of the mid-1990s, I found two articles in peer-reviewed journals (Schenk, 2009; Wade, 1998), a few dissertations, and a few book chapters or books addressing past-life therapy, none of them reporting a large-scale study of effectiveness or efficacy. In the absence of such research, past-life therapy is probably best used under the umbrella of guided imagery and, because of the unique nuances and challenges of the approach, best practiced only after training and supervision with a qualified and experienced mental health professional.

References

Jue, R. W. (1996). Past-life therapy. In B. W. Scotton, A. B. Chinen, & J. R. Battista (Eds.), *Textbook of transpersonal psychiatry and psychology* (pp. 377–387). New York, NY: Basic Books.

Lucas, W. B. (Ed.). (1993). *Regression therapy: A handbook for professionals* (Vol. 1: Past-life therapy; Vol. 2: Special instances of altered state work). Crest Park, CA: Deep Forest Press.

Moody, R. A., Jr. (1990). *Coming back: A psychiatrist explores past-life journeys*. New York, NY: Bantam Books.

Noyes, R., Fenwick, P., Holden, J. M., & Christian, R. (2009). Aftereffects of pleasurable Western adult near-death experiences. In J. M. Holden, B. Greyson, & D. James (Eds.), *The handbook of near-death experiences: Thirty years of investigation* (pp. 41–62). Santa Barbara, CA: Praeger/ABC-CLIO.

Schenk, P. W. (2009). Family systems therapy in the fourth dimension: A theoretical model for therapy of the past life type. *Australian Journal of Clinical & Experimental Hypnosis, 37*(2), 192–217.

Stevenson, I. (1974). *Twenty cases suggestive of reincarnation* (2nd ed.). Charlottesville, VA: University of Virginia Press.

Stevenson, I. (1997). *Where reincarnation and biology intersect*. Westport, CT: Praeger.

Stevenson, I. (2001). *Children who remember previous lives: A question of reincarnation* (Rev. ed.). Jefferson, NC: McFarland.

Stevenson, I. (2003). *European cases of the reincarnation type.* Jefferson, NC: McFarland.

Wade, J. (1998). The phenomenology of near-death consciousness in past-life regression therapy: A pilot study. *Journal of Near-Death Studies, 17*(1), 31–35.

Wambach, H. (1993). Appendix B: Group induction. In W. B. Lucas (Ed.), *Regression therapy: A handbook for professionals* (Vol. 1: Past-life therapy; pp. 559–564). Crest Park, CA: Deep Forest Press.

Weiss, B. L. (1988). *Many lives, many masters.* New York, NY: Fireside.

Weiss, B. L. (1993). *Through time into healing,* New York, NY: Fireside.

Weiss, B. L. (1996). *Past-life therapy professional training* (unpublished manual).

Weiss, B. L. (2012). *Miracles happen: The transformational healing power of past-life memories.* New York, NY: HarperCollins.

Woolger, R. J. (1988). *Other lives, other selves.* New York, NY: Doubleday.

Woolger, R. J. (2004). *Healing your past lives: Exploring the many lives of the soul.* Boulder, CO: Sounds True.

Zingrone, N. L., & Alvarado, C. S. (2009). Pleasurable Western adult near-death experiences: Features, circumstances, and incidence. In J. M. Holden, B. Greyson, & D. James (Eds.), *The handbook of near-death experiences: Thirty years of investigation* (pp. 17–40). Santa Barbara, CA: Praeger/ABC-CLIO.

Psychosynthesis and Dis-Identification

Janice Miner Holden

Psychosynthesis is a psychotherapeutic system rich in techniques. Roberto Assagioli (1888–1975), the Italian psychiatrist who originated psychosynthesis, listed over 60 techniques used in the approach (1965, pp. 62–64). In this chapter, I will describe one of his techniques aimed at facilitating spiritual synthesis. To aid in understanding the context of the technique, a brief overview of psychosynthesis follows.

History and Theory

With psychosynthesis, Assagioli (1965) attempted to integrate the perspectives of the numerous psychologists of his time, including Freud, Jung, Maslow, and cognitive researchers. He illustrated his view of the structure of the human psyche with his "egg diagram": an ovoid, "sitting" on end, divided horizontally into thirds (Assagioli, 1965, pp. 17–21). In the very center of the ovoid was the conscious self or "I," "the point of pure self-awareness" (Assagioli, 1965, p. 18) surrounded by a "yolk" of the field of consciousness—the contents of consciousness of which one is immediately aware. The remainder of the central section is the middle unconscious, similar to the preconscious of psychoanalysis—contents of which one can become fairly easily aware simply by directing one's attention to them. Also related to psychoanalysis was the lower third of the ovoid, the lower unconscious that "houses" various functions and manifestations: basic psychophysical functions and their related drives and complexes; "lower" parapsychological processes; pathological manifestations including phobias, compulsions, and paranoia; and dreams that were manifestations of these various features. The top third, the higher unconscious, houses the higher urges including altruistic love, genius, the potential for contemplative states of expanded consciousness, higher psychic processes, and other spiritual energies and manifestations. At the top-most point of the egg is the Higher Self:

"This Self is above, and unaffected by, the flow of the mind-stream or of bodily conditions . . . the personal conscious self [at the center of the 'egg'] should be considered merely . . . [Its] reflection, [Its] 'projection' in the field of the personality" (Assagioli, 1965, p. 19). "Awareness of the Self can . . . be achieved" (Assagioli, 1965, p. 19).

Assagioli (1965) believed that personality is, to one degree or another, fragmented, and that a fuller awareness of all aspects of one-self can be achieved through, first, a synthesis of the personal aspects of oneself, then a synthesis of the personal with the spiritual aspects. A basic manifestation of personality fragmentation is how the personal, conscious self is nearly always identified with temporary content or phenomena. These include functions—such as the body builder whose sense of identity is wrapped up in his physique or the professor whose sense of self is wrapped up in her mind—and roles—such as mother or minister. Such identification becomes clear when the func-tion or role becomes, for whatever reason, unavailable: The person is likely to experience a crisis and to question deeply, "If I am not *that*, then who *am* I?"

A "fundamental psychological principle . . . of . . . central impor-tance [in psychosynthesis is]: 'We are dominated by everything with which our self is identified. We can dominate and control everything from which we dis-identify ourselves'" (Assagioli, 1965, p. 111). Assa-gioli was not speaking here of domination and control of external people, things, or circumstances but, rather, of aspects of one's own personality to which one has non-consciously become identified. By dis-identifying from those aspects, one is liberated from their control, and one becomes, literally, "freed up" to experience one's true iden-tity as the Higher Self. In this way, one is able to become more of who one actually is. Simultaneously, rather than being tossed and turned by identification with this and then that phenomenon of experience, when one is identified as one's true nature, which is pure awareness, one has greater ability to *use* the vehicles of personality—the body, emotions, and thoughts—toward higher ends.

Assagioli (1965) described a dis-identification technique to achieve this awareness. Other proponents of psychosynthesis (Brown, 2004; Ferrucci, 2009) have developed their own variations. Most recently, contemporary philosopher and theoretical psychologist Ken Wilber (1998) referred to it as "the witness exercise," a central technique of his Integral approach. Assagioli (1965) considered this technique "a preliminary exercise helping towards a more effective use of all the other techniques [of psychosynthesis]" (p. 124). Because research on the technique has not been published, it fits the American Counseling Association's (2014) ethical designation as a "developing or innovative [technique/procedure/modality]" (p. 10, standard C.7.a.), which requires counselors to exercise relevant ethical practice such as informing clients of that designation.

The Technique

The purpose of this technique is to discriminate between the *contents* of awareness and *awareness itself*—to begin to intuit or experience the conscious (Assagioli, 1965) or transpersonal (Wilber, 1998) self, that which *is, prior to* sensation, action, thought, or emotion—that which is a center of pure awareness, pure consciousness. As with many introspective pursuits aimed at spiritual process, this exercise is probably best undertaken in a quiet, non-distracting environment, perhaps sitting comfortably, and with the eyes closed. For the first several times the exercise is done, hearing someone say the words or, if alone, listening to a previously made recording, are probably most helpful—until one has a fairly clear memory of the exercise. As one listens, one earnestly seeks to realize what the words of the exercise are getting at. One pauses between each of the sections—seen below as the paragraphs—of the exercise and takes as much time as one needs to enhance that realization. One seeks to realize that

> I have *a body, but I* am not *my body. My bodily sensations change from moment to moment. My body is sometimes ill, sometimes healthy. It has changed in appearance throughout my life and will continue to change. But that which is* aware *of changing bodily sensations, is* aware *of changing bodily health conditions, is* aware *of changing bodily appearances—that* awareness *remains constant and unchanged.* I am that awareness *that* observes *the changing conditions of my body. Being that awareness, I realize that I* have *a body, but I* am not *my body.*
>
> I have *emotions, but I* am not *my emotions. My emotions change from moment to moment. My emotions are sometimes pleasurable, sometimes distressing, sometimes even contradictory or conflicting. But that which is* aware *of changing emotions,*

whether pleasurable, distressing, contradictory, even conflicting—that awareness remains constant and unchanged. I am that awareness that observes my changing emotions. Being that awareness, I realize that I have emotions, but I am not my emotions.

I have thoughts, but I am not my thoughts. My thoughts move and change in a constant stream throughout the day and night. I can observe my stream of thoughts from a position of pure awareness. In some moments, I might even experience being that pure awareness without any particular thought. And that constant and unchanging awareness—I am that. Being that awareness, I realize that I have thoughts, but I am not my thoughts.

Having affirmed that I have a body but am not my body, that I have emotions but am not my emotions, that I have thoughts but am not my thoughts, I realize that I am a center of pure consciousness, of pure awareness. This is my essence, this still, lucid, witnessing center.

Realizing oneself as a center of pure consciousness, pure awareness, one is in a position to be more attuned to the Higher Self and its more immediate manifestation, the higher unconscious, with its higher motives that, as the Christian Bible words it, yields the "fruits of the spirit": love, joy, peace, patience, kindness, goodness, faithfulness, gentleness, and self-control. With these higher motives, one can nurture and direct the vehicles of the personality—body, emotions, and thoughts. The personality vehicles cannot, for long, be bullied or forced into higher service. But from a deeply realized position of still, pure awareness, one then can have greater access to higher inspirations and motivations, and with those higher motives, one can realize the value of the personality vehicles as one's instruments of expression and action in the world, foster their wellbeing, and bring them increasingly into the service of that which is higher—more spiritual.

Indications and Contraindications

Assagioli (1965) considered this technique appropriate for most clients. He believed it especially helpful for people strongly identified with a particular emotional state, idea, plan of action, or role; people who are overly intellectual, that is, strongly identified with their minds; and people strongly identified with their image of themselves. However, it is very appropriate for anyone who is basically mentally healthy and seeking to move toward greater spiritual realization.

Assagioli (1965) also cited contraindications: people unable to grasp the technique; those who, being in crisis, are temporarily unable to use it; people overly identified with self-observation; and people prone to withdraw into overuse of the exercise to the exclusion of effective living in the outer world. In particular, he cautioned about its use with people exhibiting borderline personality disorder or psychosis (pp. 123–124).

Wilber (1998) recommended that the dis-identification exercise be preceded by two or three minutes of his "Healing the Bodymind Split" exercise (pp. 75–84). Assagioli probably would have agreed, in that the latter exercise aims at personal synthesis as a precondition to dis-identification that facilitates transpersonal or spiritual synthesis. Both Assagioli and Wilber stated explicitly that dis-identification does not constitute ultimate Self-realization but facilitates an important step in that direction.

References

American Counseling Association. (2014). *Code of ethics.* Alexandria, VA: Author.

Assagioli, R. (1965). *Psychosynthesis: A collection of basic writings.* New York, NY: Penguin.

Brown, M. Y. (2004). *Unfolding self: The practice of psychosynthesis.* New York, NY: Allworth.

Ferrucci, P. (2009). *What we may be: Techniques for psychological and spiritual growth through psychosynthesis.* Los Angeles, CA: Jeremy P. Tarcher.

Wilber, K. (1998). *The essential Ken Wilber: An introductory reader.* Boston, MA: Shambhala.

Qigong

J. Scott Young
Jo Miller

Qigong, pronounced "chee gong," is a Chinese healing practice that is used both for self-healing and by doctors of Chinese medicine for treating disease in patients. Qigong has been described as the skill of attracting vital energy. To understand what this description means, however, it is necessary to understand that the word qigong is made up of two ideas. The first one, *Qi,* is the Chinese word for life energy and is understood in Chinese medicine as the "animating power that flows through all living things" (Cohen, 1997, p. 3). Although qi is not an idea that is easily transferable to a similar Western idea, it is something like vigor, balance, or good energy that, according to the Chinese, literally flows throughout the body and all living things. If qi is clear and flowing well, one is in an optimum state of physical and mental health. If, however, one's qi is blocked and not flowing smoothly or is polluted and dirty, one is out of balance, which causes sicknesses. The second component, *gong,* means *work.* It can also be understood as "benefits acquired through perseverance and practice" (p. 3). Therefore, the practice of qigong involves learning how to control the flow of qi energy for the purposes of optimizing physical and mind-body health.

The practice of qigong is an entire system of self-healing exercises and meditations that include healing postures, special movement exercises, self massage, breathing techniques, and special forms of meditation. Through the various exercises and methods of qigong, qi energy is accumulated and stored in the body as in a reservoir—charging the body's "bio-electrical batteries." The regular practice of qigong exercises and meditations may be helpful in strengthening the immune system and fortifying the body's vital life energy reserves to combat many different types of illness.

Two Categories

Qigong falls into two general categories: exercise and meditation. *Dong gong* is the active and dynamic form in which the entire body moves from posture to posture while the mind remains still and at rest. The practice of dong gong is what most people are referring to when they discuss qigong practice. Watching a person practicing this type of qigong looks somewhat like tai chi in that the person moves his or her body in repetitive and rhythmic movements for a period of time; however, qigong exercises are done differently than in tai chi. In qigong, there are many types of exercises that can be done to address a wide array of concerns. It is generally advisable that one only practice qigong under the supervision of a trained practitioner, as great amounts of energy can be generated from the practice and it is important to know how to utilize this energy so as not to overwhelm the system.

In *jing gong*, the entire body is motionless. Mental concentration, visualization, and precise breathing methods are employed to move qi through the body. In this approach, the mind observes the flow of qi through the body by using the breath to stimulate the movement of qi.

Why Practice Qigong?

Qigong is practiced for a number of reasons that are expressed in specific forms, yet all of these varied forms share in common the goals of balance, harmony, and the flow of qi. The forms include:

1. *Medical qigong,* used for healing and prevention of disease. Individuals highly skilled in qigong can send the qi energy out through their hands to a sick person, even at a distance of several feet. In China, many medical doctors use this practice in hospitals. Such healing is known as "external qi healing" and is considered a branch of medical qigong. Within China it is common for doctors to prescribe qigong to patients as well as other aspects of Chinese medicine such as acupuncture, herbology, and massage.
2. *External qigong,* a branch of medical qigong used to provide healing touch to cure others. External qigong is used by practitioners of Chinese medicine to give energy to patients who are sick. Masters of this approach have great control of

their own qi and can project it through their hands in the form of heat or pressure to impact the qi of another person.

3. *Meditative* or *spiritual qigong,* used for the purpose of cultivating a serene mind so that one possesses deep self-awareness and harmony with nature. Spiritual qigong arises out of both Buddhist and Taoist practices that share the goal of "a sound mind in a sound body."

4. *Confucian qigong,* used to improve one's character. This approach derives from many of the principles of Confucian teaching that when one is healthy one will behave with integrity and that those who care for themselves are more likely to care for others.

5. *Martial qigong,* used to defend and attack. This practice is related to Chinese martial arts and exercise.

Benefits of Qigong

People who practice qigong report many benefits. These may be generalized into five categories:

1. Curing illness and promoting health.
2. Enhancing vitality and developing internal force.
3. Promoting youthfulness and longevity.
4. Expanding the mind and the intellect.
5. Spiritual cultivation.

According to Chinese medical thought, practicing qigong cures, as well as prevents, all types of illness, including those considered by Western medicine to be incurable, such as asthma, diabetes, hypertension, and some cancers. It is also claimed that practicing qigong is effective for overcoming psychological problems.

Although it may seem hard to believe from a Western perspective that the practice of a set of simple rhythmic exercises can produce such results, it is important to realize that the Western medical paradigm is only one of many ways of looking at health and disease. According to models of Chinese medicine, all disease is curable. However, a particular patient may be incurable if disease has been allowed to damage the system long before treatment is sought. According to the Chinese medical perspective, illness occurs only if one or more natural human physical or psychological systems fail. Harmonious qi flow is the condition that exists when energy is balanced and flowing in an ideal state. This balanced energy then supplies the right information to every part of one's body and mind, provides the right defense or immunity, repairs all wear and tear, channels away toxic waste and negative emotions, and performs other countless acts to sustain life and health. If this harmonious chi flow is disrupted, illness occurs. The practice of qigong is to restore and enhance this harmonious qi flow (Qigong Association of America, 2013).

Clinical Applications of Qigong

Although it is unlikely that most counselors and other mental health practitioners would use qigong with their clients, it is certainly possible that qigong could be recommended as an adjunct to traditional psychotherapeutic treatments. As more Westerners become familiar with alternative treatments, it is more likely that counselors will hear clients talk about such ideas and, perhaps, request them. In general, however, counselors will be well served to have a basic knowledge of qigong, because Chinese American clients or other clients who ascribe to alternative treatments may discuss these ideas.

In the absence of publications in which researchers substantiated the frequently reported benefits of qigong, it fits the American Counseling Association's (2014) ethical designation as a "developing or innovative [technique/procedure/modality]" (p. 10, standard C.7.a.). Thus, counselors who suggest or endorse it for clients should exercise relevant ethical practice such as informing clients of that designation.

Learning about Qigong

There are now many sources for training in qigong practice in the United States. The *Qigong Research and Practice Center* in Nederland, Colorado; *The Academy of Oriental Medicine* in Austin, Texas; and the Qigong Association of America are sources for education about this approach. However, a Web search will offer many additional locations. As with venturing into any new practice, seekers are advised to inquire into the preparation and credentials of those offering the exercise of and training in the practice.

References

American Counseling Association. (2014). *Code of ethics.* Alexandria, VA: Author.

Cohen, K. S. (1997). *The way of qigong: The art and science of Chinese energy healing.* New York, NY: Ballantine Books.

Qigong Association of America. (2013). *Qigong.* Retrieved from http://www .qi.org/

Reiki

Craig S. Cashwell
Jodi L. Tangen

Just for today, do not worry.
Just for today, do not anger.
Honor your parents, teachers, and elders.
Be humble.
Respect the oneness of life.
Show gratitude.
Make your living honestly.

—Reiki Prayer

Reiki, a Japanese word, means universal life force energy. *Ki* is the Japanese variant of the Chinese *chi* or *qi*, and means life force or energy. *Rei* means universal. Depending on the belief system of the user, Reiki might be defined as God's wisdom or as the wisdom of the Earth. Regardless of what one considers the source of this energy, Reiki is the energy that animates all living things. It is the same energy that the Chinese call *chi*, Hindus call *prana*, and others refer to as *Divine Love*.

Reiki is an ancient healing art that involves the laying on of hands with intention and attunement to the universal energy life force. The Reiki practitioner, in essence, becomes a conduit for this energy and helps the client to balance the body's energy centers, facilitating the natural healing process of the body. The benefits are many and include deep relaxation, peace of mind, feelings of security and wellbeing, and expedited physical healing (Rand, 1991). Reiki is said to balance the body's energy centers (*chakras*) and to help the body heal faster. Working with the energy systems, including the chakra and meridian systems, is a common element of many well-documented therapies, including acupuncture and certain schools of massage. Reiki treatments treat the whole person—mind, body, spirit, and emotions. Mentally,

Reiki reinstates proper functioning, ranging from the cognitive to the creative. Spiritually, Reiki accesses the soul's intuition, joy, and capacity for love. The result is a body in homeostasis, a mind in equilibrium, and a soul in fulfillment (Stein, 1995).

Often described as being as old as the universe itself, Reiki as a practice was rediscovered by a Japanese monk named Dr. Mikao Usui in the late 1800s. Known to have Tibetan and Sanskrit roots, Reiki was introduced into the United States in the 1930s by a woman named Hawayo Takato. The training process is one of apprenticeship. A teacher, known as a Reiki master, passes the teaching, attunements, and symbols used for healing to a student. There are three levels of Reiki practice—First Degree, Second Degree, and Master-level—and each of these levels has a defined scope of practice. First Degree Reiki prepares the student to treat oneself and others using one's hands as they hover near the body or apply light, non-manipulative touch. Second Degree training prepares the student to access Reiki mentally for distance or absence healing. Training at the Master-level is for those who feel called to teach. Training in Reiki is available in most large communities throughout the United States. It has been embraced by persons of many diverse belief systems and religious practices.

Theoretical Foundation and Research

According to the classification designed by the National Center for Complementary and Alternative Medicine at the U.S. National Institutes of Health (NIH; as cited in Miles & True, 2003), Reiki belongs to Biofield Medicine, which involves systems that use subtle energy fields in and around the body for medical purposes. Research is ongoing in the area of Biofield Medicine (for examples, see clinicaltrials.gov). The NIH (2012) recently supported clinical trials examining the use of Reiki for prostate cancer, advanced AIDS, and fibromyalgia, among other illnesses.

There is a growing body of medical research on the benefits of Reiki, particularly in pain management, though it is still largely preliminary. Reiki therapy is practiced widely and commonly by nurse practitioners (Whelan & Wishnia, 2003) and is used in many hospital and hospice settings (Miles & True, 2003). When Reiki treatments were given to terminally ill cancer patients, results indicated periods of stabilization. These periods allowed patients time to enjoy the last days of their lives; a peaceful and calm passing if death was imminent; and relief from pain, anxiety, dyspnea, and edema (Bullock, 1997). Reiki also has been used as an adjunct treatment to opioid therapy in pain management with significant reductions in pain following the Reiki treatment (Olson & Hanson, 1997). Furthermore, Reiki has been demonstrated to be beneficial in reducing pain, mood disturbance, and fatigue in patients receiving cancer chemotherapy (Olson, Hanson, & Michaud, 2003; Post-White, Kinney, Savik Gau, Wilcox, & Lerner, 2003). Similarly, Reiki promotes comfort and restful sleep in critically ill patients (Brenner & Krenzer, 2003; Richards, Nagel, Markie, Elwell, & Barone, 2003). Reiki treatment has been shown anecdotally to enhance the treatment of HIV/AIDS (Schmehr, 2003). Beyond the reduction in symptoms, however, researchers have found that Reiki promotes comfort, calm, and wellbeing among hospitalized patients and that patients are highly satisfied with this treatment (Newshan & Schuller-Civitella, 2003). These extensive results indicate the benefits of Reiki in physical pain management.

Psychological and other physical benefits also have been documented. Engebretson and Wardell (2002) found a reduction in anxiety after Reiki treatments, and Wardell and Engebretson (2001) found a number of biological correlates of Reiki treatment, including a decrease in systolic blood pressure. There is a growing body of empirical evidence of the broad benefits of Reiki treatment, though researchers have not even begun to consider the more subtle benefits and changes that may result from Reiki treatment. Clearly, the research is in early stages, and more empirical inquiry is warranted. The majority of the research studies have been conducted using hands-on healers. In the few studies in which researchers have investigated distance or absentee healing, results have not been particularly promising.

Taken together, research findings on the use of Reiki in, or as an adjunct to, counseling are encouraging. Nevertheless, the preliminary nature of this body of work relegates Reiki to the American Counseling Association's ethical designation as a "developing or innovative [technique/procedure/modality]" (American Counseling Association, 2014, p. 10, standard C.7.a.). Thus, counselors employing or suggesting it for clients should exercise relevant ethical practice such as informing clients of that designation.

Indications

There are five ways that Reiki could be integrated into counseling practice. The first and probably least invasive way to incorporate Reiki is for counselors to use it as an adjunct to therapy. Counselors could explain the ways in which both counseling and Reiki mutually impact clients' lives and refer clients to Reiki treatment providers.

The second way that counselors can incorporate Reiki is by receiving Reiki treatment from a provider for their own self-care. Self-care and wellness are foundational elements of counseling—both for clients *and* counselors. In fact, the American Counseling Association (2013) maintains a task force to address counselor wellness and impairment. Engaging in such a personal practice may not only improve counselors' wellness but also attune them to the universal life force. Furthermore, this attunement might, in turn, improve their ability to attune to the nuances of their clients' stories.

A third way in which counselors could incorporate Reiki into counseling and further promote self-care is by learning First Degree Reiki. Furthermore, with increased knowledge of Reiki, counselors could minimally integrate comforting touch (e.g., handshakes, hugs) into the therapeutic process, always within the limits of ethical and therapeutic boundaries with clients.

Attention to ethical and physical boundaries becomes even more important if counselors choose to directly integrate Reiki treatments into the therapeutic process, which represents the fourth method of integration. It is important that counselors who employ this method first obtain full informed consent from clients and then work only within their scope of training. Such an approach could be a meaningful way to provide holistic therapy.

Finally, counselors trained in Master-level Reiki could provide psychoeducational programming that trains clients and caregivers in First Degree Reiki. This approach empowers clients to provide their own self-care, and as such, it is not unlike teaching other skills such as distress tolerance or mindfulness. Taken together, the five approaches outlined above capitalize upon the power of Reiki within the counseling context.

Cautions and Contraindications

A unique feature of Reiki is that it can be easily applied to oneself, making it a resource of self-care. There are no side effects or contraindications associated with Reiki. It is noninvasive and suitable to every age group and symptom. Because traditional Reiki treatment is a hands-on healing process, however, ethics and boundary issues are paramount when integrating this process into counseling. Approach number four above, in particular, requires informed consent from the client and particular sensitivity from the counselor to potential boundary issues. Although Reiki treatments can be provided by working with the etheric body—that is, hand placements close to the body but not physically touching—and are done with the client fully clothed, this practice still represents a physical intimacy that requires strong attention to ethics. With attention to ethics, however, Reiki can provide an important adjunct to the counseling process.

Additionally, it is important to note that research continues to develop on the effectiveness of Reiki. As such, it may not be considered an evidence-based practice and may not be covered by clients' insurance. It would be important for counselors to investigate these implications of incorporating Reiki into counseling and discuss them with their clients as well.

Henry David Thoreau once said, "What lies before us and what lies behind us are small matters compared to what lies within us. And when we bring what is within out into the world, miracles happen" (Harmonious Reiki, n.d., para. 3). The gift of Reiki resides in its power to tap into the universal life force that exists within us all. And when this life force is accessed, it may pave the way for greater healing and integration.

Suggested Resources

Print

Rand, W. L. (1991). *Reiki: The healing touch first- and second-degree manual.* Southfield, MI: Vision.

Stein, D. (1995). *Essential Reiki: A complete guide to an ancient healing art.* Freedom, CA: The Crossing Press.

Usui, M., Grimm, C. M., & Petter, F. A. (1999). *The original Reiki handbook of Dr. Mikao Usui: The traditional Usui Reiki Ryoho treatment positions and numerous Reiki techniques for health and well-being.* Twin Lakes, WI: Lotus Press.

Online

The Center for Reiki Research: http://www.centerforreikiresearch.org/

International Association of Reiki Professionals (IARP): http://www.iarp.org/

The International Center for Reiki Training: http://www.reiki.org/faq/whatisreiki.html

National Center for Complementary and Alternative Medicine: http://nccam.nih.gov/health/reiki/introduction.htm?nav=gsa

The Reiki Alliance: http://www.reikialliance.com/

References

American Counseling Association. (2013). *ACA's taskforce on counselor wellness and impairment.* Retrieved from http://www.counseling.org/knowledge-center/counselor-wellness

American Counseling Association. (2014). *Code of ethics.* Alexandria, VA: Author.

Brenner, Z. R., & Krenzer, M. E. (2003). Using complementary therapies to promote comfort at end of life. *Critical Care Nursing Clinics of North America, 15,* 355–362.

Bullock, M. (1997). Reiki: A complementary therapy for life. *American Journal of Hospice Palliative Care, 14,* 31–33.

Engebretson, J., & Wardell, D. W. (2002). Experience of a Reiki session. *Alternative Therapies in Health and Medicine, 8*(2), 48–53.

Harmonious Reiki. (n.d.). *Quotes.* Retrieved from http://www.harmoniousreiki.com/Quotes.html

Miles, P., & True, G. (2003). Reiki: Review of a biofield therapy history, theory, practice, and research. *Alternative Therapies, 9,* 62–71.

National Institutes of Health. (2012). *Clinical trials.* Retrieved from http://clinicaltrials.gov/ct2/results?term=reiki&Search=Search

Newshan, G., & Schuller-Civitella, D. (2003). Large clinical study shows value of therapeutic touch program. *Holistic Nurse Practitioner, 17*(4), 189–192.

Olson, K., & Hanson, J. (1997). Using Reiki to manage pain: A preliminary study. *Cancer Prevention Control, 1*(2), 108–113.

Olson, K., Hanson, J., & Michaud, M. (2003). A phase II trial of Reiki for the management of pain in advanced cancer patients. *Journal of Pain Symptom Management, 26,* 990–997.

Post-White, J., Kinney, M. E., Savik Gau, J. B., Wilcox, C., & Lerner, I. (2003). Therapeutic massage and healing touch improve symptoms in cancer. *Integrated Cancer Therapy, 2*(4), 332–344.

Richards, K., Nagel, C., Markie, M., Elwell, J, & Barone, C. (2003). Use of complementary and alternative therapies to promote sleep in critically ill patients. *Critical Care Nursing Clinics of North America, 15,* 329–340.

Schmehr, R. (2003). Enhancing the treatment of HIV/AIDS with Reiki training and treatment. *Alternative Therapeutic Health Medicine, 9,* 118–120.

Wardell, D. W., & Engebretson, J. (2001). Biological correlates of Reiki touch healing. *Journal of Advanced Nursing, 33*(4), 439–445.

Whelan, K. M., & Wishnia, G. S. (2003). Reiki therapy: The benefits to a nurse/Reiki practitioner. *Holistic Nurse Practitioner, 17,* 209–217.

Simplicity

THE FORGOTTEN SPIRITUAL DISCIPLINE

Jennifer M. Foster

The spiritual discipline of simplicity is defined as an internal contentment that is expressed in one's lifestyle. It fosters an authentic spiritual life, personal growth, and connection with God or a higher power. This ancient discipline may be difficult to practice in modern culture. In an age of consumerism, simplicity practices are countercultural and require self-reflection and intentionality. In this chapter, I will provide a brief history of the spiritual discipline of simplicity, an overview of common simplicity practices, theoretical and research underpinnings, suggestions for its use in counseling, and resources for further development.

Historical Overview of the Spiritual Discipline of Simplicity

The origin of the spiritual discipline of simplicity is difficult to pinpoint, as the practice has been documented in early human history. It spans multiple world religions, including Hinduism, Buddhism, and Christianity. Numerous philosophers, scholars, and spiritual leaders have written about benefits of simplicity, including Henry David Thoreau (1910), Ralph Waldo Emerson (1836), St. Francis of Assisi (1906), and Mahatma Gandhi (1927). Additionally, the teachings of Buddha as recorded in the Vinaya Pitaka and Jesus Christ as documented in the Bible have addressed the spiritual discipline of simplicity. Together these writings warn about greed and emphasize the necessity of self-discipline, moderation, contentment, and the value of nonmaterial things.

    Simplicity in the United States can be traced to American pioneers. Over time the spiritual practice has waxed and waned. In the United

States today, simplicity is practiced by both religious and nonreligious groups, including Old Order Amish, Old Order Mennonites, and voluntary simplifiers who typically identify as being spiritual but may or may not be connected to a particular religious belief system.

Although the 1960s and 1970s were characterized by several anti-consumerism movements, the modern simplicity movement is frequently attributed to Elgin (1981) and the publication of his book on the topic. He described the simplified life as one that is "outwardly simple and inwardly rich" (p. 2). Through this lifestyle, a person seeks to live in harmony with one's personal values (Chi, 2008; Mullaney, 2001). The following section details common simplicity practices.

Simplicity Practices

Individuals practice simplicity for multiple reasons. The three most commonly cited reasons are individual spirituality, personal benefit, and desire to care for the environment (Craig-Lees & Hill, 2002). To achieve these goals, individuals implement a wide range of simplicity practices (Bekin, Carrigan, & Szmigin, 2005; Elgin, 1981; Etzioni, 2004; Foster, 1998; Murray, 2005). In this section, I identify some common practices amongst this diverse group with regard to five areas: work, consumption, transportation, community connection, and parenting practices. I will also illuminate how simplicity affects each of these domains.

Reflection upon one's use of time and how well it correlates with personal values often results in work-related changes for individuals who wish to simplify. Many simplifiers reject careerism (Grigsby, 2000), which tends to place a greater emphasis on one's career goals than on relationships with others. To achieve improved work-life balance, individuals may decrease their hours, become self-employed, return to school for a more desirable career, or retire and dedicate their time to family volunteer work (Bekin et al., 2005).

In addition to work changes, individuals who practice simplicity often strive to reduce their consumption. Some people buy less and purchase items with greater ethical-mindedness. For example, individuals may purchase second-hand goods to extend the life of products (Bekin et al., 2005), shop close to home and purchase locally produced goods (Huneke, 2005), or buy only environmentally friendly items (Bekin et al.; Chi, 2008). Many simplifiers produce and process their own food.

Thoughtful spending and accumulation of goods is frequently coupled with a desire to share resources with others in need.

Along with altered consumption practices, some individuals who engage in simplicity practices change their mode of transportation. Instead of owning a vehicle, they may walk, ride bicycles, or utilize public transportation. Others who must travel farther may ride share (Bekin et al., 2005; Shaw & Newholm, 2002). Transportation changes are often financially, physically, relationally, and environmentally advantageous.

Another common simplicity practice is a deliberate effort to live in close community with others. Some relocate to tightly knit, often self-sufficient, intentional communities (Bekin et al., 2005; Chi 2008). For these groups, it is common to share aspects of everyday life, such as meals, childcare, and services. Although some people who practice simplicity seek to live with others with shared values, many remain in their current location and increase their community involvement, such as getting to know their neighbors, volunteering, and participating in a support group. Research indicates that close relationship with others is a significant factor that contributes to personal happiness (Schwartz, 2004). Many people who practice simplicity decrease work hours, long commutes, and other time-consuming commitments to increase the amount of time that they can spend with family, friends, and neighbors.

Along with developing intimate relationships, individuals who practice simplicity often alter their approach to parenting. Simple living sources encourage parents to allow their children to have free time, which is countercultural to today's over-scheduled children (Elkind, 2001; Huneke, 2005). Parents strive to spend quality time with their children and to be fully present with them. Parents may also elect to decrease their children's—as well as their own—media exposure (Huneke, 2005; Postman, 1994). Those people who practice simplicity seek contentment and aim to decrease their appetite for a constant need for more. By limiting media exposure, parents protect the social construct of childhood and teach their children other methods of attaining satisfaction.

The above practices related to work, consumption, transportation, community connection, and parenting practices are a sample of the numerous ways individuals choose to simplify. The decision to simplify involves a new way of thinking and being in the world. Reduction of activities and possessions creates space for personal, relational, and spiritual growth. The following section examines research literature related to simplicity practices.

Research Studies Exploring Simplicity Practices

Researchers of simplicity practices have identified numerous health and wellness benefits (Beecher, 2007; Bekin et al., 2005; Biswas-Diener, Vitterso, & Diener, 2005; Miller et al., 2007; Murray, 2005). Beecher's (2007) qualitative study analyzed interviews with voluntary simplifiers, which resulted in three themes regarding the simplicity lifestyle: impact on the environment, improved relationship with others, and intrapersonal benefits. The study suggested that simplicity practices may lead to improved personal wellbeing.

In a participant-observation research study, Bekin and colleagues (2005) investigated whether or not individuals who simplify achieve their personal goals through their lifestyle. Researchers visited five randomly selected, intentional communities, and participated in activities with participants such as gardening, cooking, and composting. The researchers uncovered challenges associated with the lifestyle, such as being environmentally conscious. Mobility was also an obstacle for many community members who continued to work in the general society. Despite the difficulties, participants expressed increased levels of fulfillment.

In another study, Biswas-Diener and colleagues (2005) examined the subjective wellbeing, both cognitive and affective, of three groups that practiced simplicity: the Kenyan Maasai, the United States Amish, and the Greenlandic Inughit. Each group's combined subjective wellbeing score was above the neutral point on all 54 scales. Moreover, the scores were significantly above neutral on 53 of the scales, with participants rating themselves as mildly to moderately happy.

Miller and colleagues (2007) conducted one of the first population-based assessments on Amish women. Through surveying 288 Amish women, the researchers discovered evidence of the health and wellbeing within this unique group. The researchers concluded that "Amish women rated their mental health much higher, had fewer diagnoses of depression, perceived themselves to experience less stress, less intimate partner violence, less unfair treatment due to gender, and to have had higher levels of social support" (p. 169).

A final study worthy of noting was conducted by Murray (2005) to investigate the impact of simplicity practices on physical, mental, and spiritual health. Data were collected through individual interviews, a focus group, and written wellness assessments. According to Murray, "six intertwining themes emerged as essentials mentioned by every participant: mindful living; wise use of resources; interdependence between humans, the environment, and nonhuman beings; generosity; decision for happiness and optimism; and humor" (p. 173). Participants took personal ownership for their health and wellbeing and actively worked to improve it. Murray asserted that simplification has the potential to result in numerous benefits to one's wellbeing.

Although the above studies tentatively support benefits of simplicity practices, based on the dearth of empirical literature on the topic, quantitative studies with large samples are especially needed (Brown & Krasser, 2005). Such studies could focus on the benefits and obstacles faced by those who attempt to simplify in modern cultures. Further research related to the mental health needs of those who choose a simplified lifestyle is also needed for both simplifiers in mainstream culture and those who reside in separate communities (Cates, 2005; Cates & Graham, 2002; Snyder & Bowman, 2004).

Integration of the Spiritual Discipline of Simplicity into Counseling

Simplicity practices can be incorporated into counseling to improve wellness and restore balance. More than one in four Americans reported feeling lonely (Schwartz, 2004), and increased levels of isolation may be linked to depression (Putnam, 2000). Today's clients often report feeling exhausted, experience a lack of contentment, and find difficulty connecting with others. It is possible that such clients may benefit from simplicity exercises, which may lead to greater inner peace and connection to one's spiritual self as well as others.

Clients who indicate a desire to simplify can start by taking an inventory of their lives. With the guidance of their counselors, they may be asked to rate their wellbeing in five domains: social, emotional, physical, mental, and spiritual. Clients also need to clarify their core values. Following a multidimensional assessment, counselors can help clients explore changes that they would like to make to attain their personal goals. Counselors and clients could then collaborate to design exercises to help foster the desired changes. Over time, counselors and clients monitor progress and explore challenges.

A variety of exercises exist to help and challenge clients to simplify their lives. Some of these challenges are small and can be implemented quickly, whereas others require more significant change over a longer period of time. Counselors can help clients explore their readiness for change as well as feelings of ambivalence regarding a different lifestyle.

Some starter exercises may involve reducing media exposure and taking breaks from technology, such as social media and email. To take this exercise a step further, clients can be challenged to invest the time formerly spent watching television or using the Internet on fostering relationships with family, friends, and neighbors. Clients may also experiment with using additional time to give back to their communities through volunteering. Solitude, meditation, and reflective practices to slow down one's pace and focus on one's center can also be recommended as small steps that have the potential to lead to significant changes over time. Gratitude practices may also be recommended to focus on blessings and reduce searching for items to feel good and fill a void (Schwartz, 2004). A final starter exercise is to change one's typical mode of entertainment (e.g., movie, concert, dinner out) to a free activity, conducted if possible in nature, such visiting a local park or hiking a trail.

Over time some clients may indicate that they are ready to make some larger-scale changes. For example, clients may assess how well their current job aligns with their values. Clients may wish to reduce their hours, pursue a different occupation, or become self-employed. Another large change may be in the area of personal finances. Clients may decide to evaluate their current spending and create an updated budget. A different view about money may enable clients to be satisfied with less, to differentiate between wants and needs, to decrease impulse buying, and if desired to increase their charitable giving. Clients may reconsider their current mode of transportation and choose public transportation or ride sharing. They may also experiment with buying second-hand goods or borrowing items when needed instead of owning them.

It is important to highlight some cautions for the use of simplicity practices in counseling. First, the research on simplicity and its benefits is still developing (Huneke, 2005). Although simplicity has been investigated in the fields of religion, sociology, anthropology, and marketing

(Bekin et al., 2005), it has only recently been explored in the counseling and psychology literature (Iwata, 2006). Thus, it fits the American Counseling Association's (2014) ethical designation as a "developing or innovative [technique/procedure/modality]" (p. 10, standard C.7.a.), which requires counselors to exercise relevant ethical practice such as informing clients of that designation. Second, when individuals decrease their consumer tendencies, it leaves a void that must be filled (Etzioni, 2004). As a result, clients may feel anxious and resort to negative coping mechanisms. Etzioni suggested that people in the process of simplifying need encouragement from others. Lastly, the spiritual discipline of simplicity is meant to be an expression of inward change. Without an inward focus, the tasks may result in a legalistic approach to one's spirituality. There is not one right way to practice this discipline, and individuals are best advised to be nonjudgmental of themselves and others in this process.

In conclusion, although limited research exists on the spiritual discipline of simplicity, some evidence appears to support its enhancement of health and wellbeing (Beecher, 2007; Bekin et al., 2005; Biswas-Diener et al., 2005; Miller et al., 2007; Murray, 2005). Its practice has the potential to benefit both counselors and their clients as they strive for balance, inner peace, and greater connection with others as well as with God or a Higher Power.

Suggested Resources

Print

Andrews, C. (1997). *The circle of simplicity: Return to the good life.* New York, NY: Harper Collins.

Dominguez, J., & Robin, V. (1992). *Your money or your life: Transforming your relationship with money and achieving financial independence.* New York, NY: Viking Penguin.

Elgin, D. (1981). *Voluntary simplicity.* New York, NY: William Morrow.

Foster, R. J. (1998). *Celebration of discipline: The path to spiritual growth.* New York, NY: HarperCollins.

Payne, K. J., & Ross, L. M. (2010). *Simplicity parenting: Using the extraordinary power of less to raise calmer, happier, and more secure kids.* New York, NY: Ballantine Books.

Pierce, L. B. (2000). *Choosing simplicity: Real people finding peace and fulfillment in a complex world.* Carmel, CA: Gallagher Press.

Online

Becoming Minimalist: http://www.becomingminimalist.com/
Center for a New American Dream: http://www.newdream.org/
Financial Integrity: http://www.financialintegrity.org/
Intentional Communities: http://www.ic.org
Slow Your Home: http://www.slowyourhome.com/

References

American Counseling Association. (2014). *Code of ethics.* Alexandria, VA: Author.

Assisi, F. (1906). *The writings of Saint Francis of Assisi.* (P. Robinson, Trans.). Philadelphia, PA: Dolphin Press.

Beecher, T. S. (2007). *Questioning the consumer culture: A qualitative study on voluntary simplicity* (Doctoral dissertation). Retrieved from http://www.proquest.com (Order No. 3294608).

Bekin, C., Carrigan, M., & Szmigin, I. (2005). Defying marketing sovereignty: Voluntary simplicity at new consumption communities. *Qualitative Market Research: An International Journal, 8*(4), 413–429.

Biswas-Diener, R., Vitterso, J., & Diener, E. (2005). Most people are pretty happy, but there is cultural variation: The Inughuit, the Amish, and the Maasai. *Journal of Happiness Studies, 6*(3), 205–226.

Brown, K. W., & Krasser, T. (2005). Are psychological and ecological wellbeing compatible? The role of values, mindfulness and lifestyle. *Social Indicators Research, 74,* 349–368.

Cates, J. A. (2005). Facing away: Mental health treatment with the Old Order Amish. *American Journal of Psychotherapy, 59*(4), 371–383.

Cates, J. A., & Graham, L. L. (2002). Psychological assessment of the Old Order Amish: Unraveling the enigma. *Professional Psychology: Research and Practice, 33*(2), 155–161.

Chi, K. R. (2008). *The motivations and challenges of living simply in a consuming society* (Master's thesis). Retrieved from http://www.proquest.com (Order No. 1452963).

Craig-Lees, M., & Hill, C. (2002). Understanding voluntary simplifiers. *Psychology & Marketing, 19*(2), 187–210.

Elkind, D. (2001). *The hurried child: Growing up too fast too soon* (3rd ed.). Cambridge, MA: Perseus.

Emerson, R. W. (1836). *Nature.* Boston, MA: J. Munroe.

Etzioni, A. (2004). The post-affluent society. *Review of Social Economy, 62*(3), 407–420.

Gandhi, M. K. (1927). *An autobiography: Or, the story of my experiments with truth.* (M. H. Desai, Trans.). Ahmedabad, India: Navajivan.

Grigsby, M. E. (2000). *Buying time and getting by: The voluntary simplicity movement* (Doctoral dissertation). Retrieved from http://www.proquest .com (Order No. 9974635).

Huneke, M. E. (2005). The face of the un-consumer: An empirical examination of the practice of voluntary simplicity in the United States. *Psychology & Marketing, 22*(7), 527–550.

Iwata, O. (2006). An evaluation of consumerism and lifestyle as correlates of a voluntary simplicity lifestyle. *Social Behavior and Personality, 34*(5), 557–568.

Miller, K., Yost, B., Flaherty, S., Hillemeier, M. M., Chase, G. A., Weisman, C. S., et al. (2007). Health status, health conditions, and health behaviors among Amish women: Results from the central Pennsylvania women's health study. *Women's Health Issues, 17*(3), 162–171.

Mullaney, T. J. (2001). *Voluntary simplicity: An enacted reality* (Doctoral dissertation). Retrieved from http://www.proquest.com (Order No. 3003257).

Murray, M. C. (2005). *Simple wellness: Perceptions of health in persons who practice voluntary simplicity* (Doctoral dissertation). Retrieved from http://www.proquest.com (Order No. 3221511).

Postman, N. (1994). *The disappearance of childhood.* New York, NY: Vintage Books.

Putnam, R. D. (2000). *Bowling alone: The collapse and revival of American community.* New York, NY: Simon & Schuster.

Schwartz, B. (2004). *The paradox of choice: Why more is less.* New York, NY: Harper Perennial.

Shaw, D., & Newholm, T. (2002). Voluntary simplicity and the ethics of consumption. *Psychology and Marketing, 19*(2), 167–185.

Snyder, L., & Bowman, S. (2004). Communities in cooperation: Human services work with Old Order Mennonites. *Journal of Ethnic & Cultural Diversity in Social Work, 13*(2), 91–118.

Thoreau, H. D. (1910). *Thoreau's Walden.* New York, NY: Longmans, Green.

Sprint with Spirit

Running as a Spiritual Intervention in Counseling

R. Lewis Bozard Jr.

Running—one of the most primitive and invigorating physical activities of the human experience—is easily recognized as a body-oriented practice. Furthermore, abundant research has demonstrated mental health benefits of running, from alleviation of depressive symptoms to enhanced cognition (Hays, 1999; Huang, Norman, Zabinski, Calfas, & Patrick, 2007; Joosse, Stearns, Anderson, Hartlaub, & Euclide, 2008). Perhaps less apparent is the additional potential for running to be applied as a meaningful spiritual practice. Running may be utilized in conjunction with counseling to enhance outcomes through integration of body, mind, and spirit.

Running as Therapeutic

Running is a popular fitness activity, as evidenced by the increasing numbers of participants in organized running events in recent years. Active.com (2011) reported that between 2008 and 2010, marathon race participation increased by 203%, half-marathon race participation increased 154%, 10K race participation grew by 155%, and 5K race participation rose by 144%. Running emerged as a popular exercise activity in the United States during the "running boom" of the 1960s and 1970s. Many people may have a basic awareness that running provides some level of psychological benefit, ranging from stress reduction to heightened psychic energy and alertness. However, the potential for the integration of running with counseling is less known both to the general public and many practitioners.

Connections between physical activity and mental wellbeing have been acknowledged since at least ancient Greece (Hays, 1999). Greist and colleagues (1979) in their study of the use of running in the treatment of depression wrote powerfully that "depressive cognitions and affect seldom emerge during running, and when they do, they are virtually impossible to maintain" (p. 45). Hays (1999) reported that exercise may be an effective modality of treatment for some individuals experiencing the following mental health-related conditions: depression; anxiety; stress, low self-esteem and mastery issues; disordered eating; substance abuse recovery; body image disturbance; chronic mental illness; empowerment of trauma survivors; and recovery from medical illness. Cognitive self-perceptions of the exerciser may change, usually for the better, as a result of participation in exercise (Huang, Norman, Zabinski, Calfas, & Patrick, 2007; Joosse et al., 2008). For example, as a result of exercise clients may perceive themselves to be more successful, healthier, more desirable, and/or more attractive. Exercise may produce a positive effect by diverting cognitive attention, either purposefully or coincidentally, away from destructive thoughts and actions (Hays, 1999). Chronic exercise, which occurs in repetition on a regular basis, has been shown to produce more significant and enduring effects than acute, or short-term, bouts of exercise (Buckworth & Dishman, 2002).

Running as Counseling Intervention

Running will not be an appropriate intervention for every client. In fact, running will not be appropriate or desired by the majority of clients in most counseling settings. However, for clients who already have experience with running and find it enjoyable, or at least tolerable, or for clients with an interest in beginning a program of running, the intervention may be highly effective. Before recommending that any client who has not been exercising begin to do so, the counselor should direct the client to seek medical consultation to ensure that the client may safely increase physical activity (Hays, 1999).

Factors that may contraindicate running as an intervention include serious medical conditions, a history of exercise addiction, lack of interest in exercise, obsessive-compulsive symptomology, and severe depression and/or suicidal ideation (Sachs & Buffone, 1984). Hays (1999) cautioned that the mental health professional should not assume the role of trainer or coach. Rather, mental health outcomes and wellness aspects of exercise should be the specific focus of mental health counselors (Okonski, 2003). Counselors who apply exercise interventions without proper awareness of the nature and risks of exercise may open themselves to the possibility of ethical and/or legal liability if clients are harmed physically or psychologically (Dixon, Mauzey, & Hall, 2003; Hays, 1999).

Running may be applied as a counseling intervention that is either adjunctive to therapy or a medium of therapy (Hays, 1999). When the client runs outside of counseling sessions, exercise is adjunctive to therapy. When the counselor runs with the client during counseling sessions, exercise is a medium of therapy (Hays, 1999; Kostrubala, 1984). Exercise as an adjunct modality is the more frequently applied approach (Hays, 1999). The adjunctive modality is also in most cases preferable when spirituality is an explicitly desired element of running, as this approach will allow the client to focus with minimal distractions. When qualified to do so, a counselor using an adjunct approach may act in the role of consultant, offering both encouragement and technical advice. He or she may administer to the client what is called an exercise prescription—a directive to exercise at a certain level of intensity for a certain period of time at a specified frequency—as part of the client's clinical treatment plan (Buckworth & Dishman, 2002). The purpose of the prescription may be to achieve a specific treatment goal such as weight reduction, or the prescription may be given to improve symptoms such as anxiety or depression (Hays, 1999).

Running as Spiritual

Concerning the relationship between sports and spirituality, Catholic theologian Michael Novak (1992) wrote:

> Sports are religious in the sense that they are organized institutions, disciplines, liturgies; and also in the sense that they teach religious qualities of heart and soul. In particular, they recreate symbols of cosmic struggle, in which human survival and moral courage are not assured. To this extent, they are not mere games, diversions, pastimes. Their power to exhilarate or depress is far greater than that. (p. 36)

The ancient Greek Olympic games, in which running constituted a primary event, served in part to honor the gods, attributing to running an explicitly spiritual purpose (Fry, 2007). Running in contemporary times "becomes religious [spiritual] in a robust sense when one infuses the experience—not unnaturally—with a religious [spiritual] meaning and purpose" (Fry, 2007, p. 69).

Running may be applied as an explicitly spiritual intervention in counseling by giving specific attention to the roles of meaning and purpose along with the physical activity. Although spiritual elements and practices associated with running may be limitless, nine are offered here as examples. Many have been experienced directly by the author, whereas others originate from external sources.

Prayer and meditation

The client may use running as an opportunity for contemplation, meditative focus, or prayer, especially when running occurs in a setting that is relatively quiet with minimal distractions; runs in busy urban settings, for example, may be less effective or hazardous if the runner does not maintain sharp awareness of dangers such as moving vehicles in one's path.

Rhythm and repetition

In much the same way that rosary beads utilize repetition to intensify spiritual focus, running provides opportunities for spiritual centering through rhythm and repetition. Patterns emerge during a run through breathing and movement of the feet, legs, and arms. The rhythm of breath and movement may induce a state of heightened mental and spiritual focus as the client relaxes his or her mind and experiences the familiar repetition.

Perseverance

Running may provide a body-centric experience of perseverance—training toward a goal and following through on the plan—that can promote perseverance in other areas salient to counseling, such as enduring challenges related to work, relationships, or grief/loss.

Connection with nature

Many runners value their activity as an opportunity to be outdoors and experience the natural world. Awareness of one's place in the universe, as part of larger whole, may be reassuring to the client. The sensual experience of the bright, warm sun on one's body, the dampness of a run in the rain, or the sharp sting of a cold winter wind on exposed skin, although potentially unpleasant, stimulate the body and highlight the interplay between human existence and the forces of nature.

Self-discipline/asceticism

The spiritual practice of self-discipline coincides with an organized approach to running. The client who takes running seriously will require the self-discipline to get out and run even when he or she does not feel the desire to do so. The closely related self-denial practiced in conjunction with running, as when one selects healthy and energizing foods over junk foods, speaks to the longstanding spiritual value of asceticism.

Sacred space/retreat

Runners commonly utilize their sport as a form of escape, a method to get away from the stresses and strains of daily life, if only for 20–30 minutes. Similarly, running may be viewed as an opportunity for spiritual retreat in sacred space. The run may be the best opportunity in the day or the week to find spiritual rest and renewal.

Mindfulness

Running presents opportunities for appreciation of often-overlooked elements of one's existence. During a run, the client may choose to focus on mindful awareness of the life-giving act of breathing, for example. The running client may alternatively focus mindfully using a chant (Joslin, 2003).

Pilgrimage

Running, unless it occurs on a treadmill, involves a physical journey, moving from one place to another. With conscious awareness, the client may similarly experience a run as a spiritual pilgrimage, a holy and meaningful journey of both body and spirit during which the transcendent and the existential may be encountered (Joslin, 2003; Kay, 2007).

Altered/heightened states of consciousness

During the activity of running, many people experience transport to altered or heightened states of consciousness (Fry, 2007). Such states facilitate self-transcendence, rising to a place of being beyond the ordinary experience of the self. A common example is the phenomenon of "runner's high." The condition involves feelings of relaxation and ecstasy that enhance mood states long after the exercise has ended. The release of endorphins has long been theorized as the cause of runner's high, and Boecker and colleagues (2008) discovered a positive relationship between the experience of runner's high and the release of endogenous opioids in the frontolimbic area of the brain.

Conclusion

Applied selectively with appropriate clients, running as a counseling intervention integrating body, mind, and spirit can produce significant, positive, and enduring effects to enhance counseling outcomes. Although this article has focused specifically on running, similar applications might be possible using other forms of exercise such as swimming, walking, yoga, and weight lifting. Counselors should consider harnessing the power of running to benefit clients in ways neither the counselor nor the client imagined possible.

Suggested Resources

Print

Austin, M. W. (Ed.) (2007). *Running and philosophy: A marathon for the mind*. Malden, MA: Blackwell.

Chung, Y. B., & Baird, M. K. (1999). Physical exercise as a counseling intervention. *Journal of Mental Health Counseling, 21*(2), 124–135.

Dixon, W. A., Mauzey, E. D., & Hall, C. R. (2003). Physical activity and exercise: Implications for counselors. *Journal of Counseling and Development, 81*, 502–505.

Hays, K. F. (1999). *Working it out: Using exercise in psychotherapy.*
Washington, DC: American Psychological Association.

Joslin, R. D. (2003). *Running the spiritual path: A runner's guide to breathing,
meditating, and exploring the prayerful dimension of the sport.* New York,
NY: St. Martin's Press.

Kay, W. A. (2007). *Running—the sacred art: Preparing to practice.*
Woodstock, VT: SkyLight Paths.

Kostrubala, T. (1976). *The joy of running.* New York, NY: Lippincott.

Sachs, M. L., & G. W. Buffone (Eds.). (1984). *Running as therapy: An
integrated approach.* Lincoln, NE: University of Nebraska Press.

Sacks, M. H., & Sachs, M. L. (Eds.). (1981). *Psychology of running.*
Champaign, IL: Human Kinetics.

References

Active.com. (2011). *Active network tracks surge in US running event
participation.* Retrieved from http://www.activenetwork.com/about-us/
press-room/press-releases/2011-press-releases/active-network-tracks
-surge-in-US-running-event-participation.htm

Boecker, H., Sprenger, T., Spilker, M. E., Henriksen, G., Koppenhoefer, M.,
Wagner, K. J. . . . Tolle, T. R. (2008). The runner's high: Opioidergic
mechanisms in the human brain. *Cerebral Cortex, 18*(11), 2523–2531.

Buckworth, J., & Dishman, R. K. (2002). *Exercise psychology.* Champaign, IL:
Human Kinetics.

Fry, J. P. (2007). Running religiously. In M. W. Austin (Ed.), *Running
and philosophy: A marathon for the mind* (pp. 57–70). Malden, MA:
Blackwell.

Greist, J. H., Klein, M. H., Eischens, R. R., Faris, J., Gurman, A. S., &
Morgan, W. P. (1979). Running as treatment for depression. *Journal of
Comparative Psychiatry, 20,* 41–54.

Hays, K. F. (1999). *Working it out: Using exercise in psychotherapy.*
Washington, DC: American Psychological Association.

Huang J. S., Norman G. J., Zabinski M. F., Calfas K., & Patrick K. (2007).
Body image and self-esteem among adolescents undergoing an
intervention targeting dietary and physical activity behaviors. *Journal of
Adolescent Health, 40,* 245–251.

Joosse, L., Stearns, M., Anderson, H., Hartlaub, P., & Euclide, J. (2008). Fit
Kids/Fit Families: A report on a countywide effort to promote healthy
behaviors. *Wisconsin Medical Journal, 107*(5), 231–237.

Kostrubala, T. (1984). Running and therapy. In M. L. Sachs & G. W. Buffone
    (Eds.), *Running as therapy: An integrated approach* (pp. 112–124).
    Lincoln, NE: University of Nebraska Press.

Novak, M. (1992). The natural religion. In S. J. Hoffman (Ed.), *Sport and
    religion* (pp. 35–55). Champaign, IL: Human Kinetics.

Okonski, V. O. (2003). Exercise as a counseling intervention. *Journal of
    Mental Health Counseling, 25,* 45–56.

Transpersonal Experiences

RESPONDING
THERAPEUTICALLY

Janice Miner Holden

From an expanded definition offered by Stanislav Grof (1976; 1985, pp. 66ff.), transpersonal experiences are spontaneous, usually transient experiences involving perception and/or action that *transcends* the usual *personal* limits of space, time, and/or identity yet, paradoxically, are perceived as authentic or potentially authentic by the experiencer with consensus reality testing intact (Fall, Holden, & Marquis, 2010, p. 433). Authors have referred to some or all of these experiences by other terms, such as religious experiences (James, 1902/1990), spiritually transformative experiences (STEs; Kason, 2008), potentially spiritually transformative experiences (pSTEs; Holden, Kinsey, & Moore, 2014), and anomalous experiences (Cardeña, Lynn, & Krippner, 2000). Rhea White's (2001) list of "Exceptional Human Experiences" consists predominantly, but not entirely, of transpersonal experiences. People throughout history and across cultures have reported such experiences (Cardeña et al., 2000; Kellehear, 2009).

One way to categorize transpersonal experiences is as intuitive, paranormal, and transmaterial. Intuitive experiences are those in which the experiencer has a "knowing" about something or someone that the experiencer cannot attribute to sensory input or rational process (Fall et al., 2010, p. 434). A child comes home one day and reports to her parent that she made a new friend at school; the parent suddenly has a "bad feeling" that this new friend is somehow "trouble"—a feeling that is borne out over the coming weeks. At a party, two single strangers' eyes meet across the room, and both feel something unusual and positive; they introduce themselves, and within weeks they are in a committed relationship with the mutual sense that they are "soul mates."

Paranormal experiences paradoxically involve the material world in some way and also seem to defy established physical laws of that world

(Fall et al., 2010, p. 434). Receptive paranormal experiences involve knowledge that seems to occur in the absence of physical sensory input or rational deduction. They include telepathy—knowing the feelings, thoughts, or experiences of another person who is either close by or at a great distance; precognition—knowing that something is going to happen; clairvoyance—envisioning something outside the range of one's sensory perception; and out-of-body experiences—perceiving one's consciousness to be functioning apart from the physical body. Active paranormal experiences include telekinesis—the movement of objects in the absence of detectable physical force, and psychic healing—the improvement of a problematic physical condition without direct physical intervention or without recognized standard or alternative interventions. Most paranormal phenomena occur unintentionally, but even when facilitated by intention they remain essentially spontaneous, that is, outside the complete control of the experiencer.

Transmaterial experiences include perception of transmaterial entities and environments—those not of the material world—and sometimes communication with such entities. These include after-death communication—in which a living person perceives and may communicate with a deceased person—and mystical experiences—in which the experiencer communes with a non-material entity perceived to be of a higher or spiritual nature.

Several questions typically arise regarding transpersonal experiences. Among these are whether the experiences are more than subjectively real. Some researchers have approached this question by contrasting the phenomenology of transpersonal experiences with predominantly "purely subjective" experiences such as hallucinations or dreams and finding them to be essentially different (Sartori, 2004). Others have examined veridical—that is, objectively verifiable—aspects of certain transpersonal experiences and found predominant accuracy of perception; included were both paranormal and transmaterial perceptions, the latter cases involving perception of deceased people not yet known to have died (Greyson, 2010; Holden et al., 2009). Yet others have reviewed the extensive experimental research on paranormal experiences and concluded that findings support the reality of these phenomena (Beauregard, 2012; Powell, 2009; Radin, 1997, 2006; Targ, 2012; Tart, 2009).

A further question is the extent and range of aftereffects of transpersonal experiences. In the aftermath of some transpersonal experiences, people report and are observed to have experienced temporary and sometimes lasting aftereffects (Holden, 2013). These aftereffects range from immediate to delayed, from mild to profound, and from ease to difficulty of integration. They can manifest in the biological, psychological, spiritual, and/or social domains, and they usually manifest in an overlapping way in more than one domain. In general, the more detailed, prolonged, and intense the transpersonal experience, the greater the likelihood of aftereffects. Although a complete summary of potential aftereffects is beyond the scope of this paper, an example from each domain is: biological—changes in needs and appetites for food, sleep, and sex; psychological—loss of fear of death; spiritual—increased paranormal phenomena such as precognition and telepathy; and social—changes in marital partners, friends, and careers. Sometimes these aftereffects manifest as seemingly permanent changes that constitute development: stable functioning in a more inclusive and adaptive mode than was the case prior to the experience (Foster & Holden, 2010).

Another common question is whether transpersonal experiences are related to or a manifestation of mental disorder. Research from a variety of sources indicates that the answer is no: that these are "equal opportunity" experiences, occurring to people across the mental health spectrum and not, in and of themselves, an indication of mental disorder (Noble, 1987; Noyes, Fenwick, Holden, & Christian, 2009; Streit-Horn, 2011). However, an influx of transpersonal experiences in an amount too great and/or form too foreign for a person to easily integrate psychologically can manifest in dysfunction—disabling feelings and difficulty functioning—a condition sometimes termed spiritual emergency (Grof & Grof, 1989; Holden, VanPelt, & Warren, 1999). Yvonne Kason (2008) summarized criteria for distinguishing spiritual emergency from psychosis:

> If a person can distinguish between inner and outer experiences, is clearly aware of which inner experiences do not fit into the prevailing world view of reality, is able to function in the world, is able to make discerning judgments, and has appropriate control of his or her emotions, he or she is, by definition, not psychotic. This is true no matter how unusual or bizarre the inner experiences may seem. (p. 247)

People often report that their transpersonal experiences are among the most meaningful in their lives (Noyes et al., 2009); at the same time, because these experiences contradict the materialist, reductionist philosophy that dominates Western culture, the experiencer may feel challenged to integrate the experience and its aftereffects into a coherent sense of self. Thus, talking with someone helpful can be an important aspect of the integration process (Foster et al., 2009; Grof & Grof, 1989; Kason, 2008). Conversely, near-death experiencers (NDErs) and other transpersonal experiencers have described feeling harmed as a result of disclosing their experiences to healthcare professionals. In a recent study of 89 NDErs reporting on their most memorable 189 experiences of disclosure (Holden et al., 2014), although on average they found those experiences to be more helpful than harmful, they reported extremely harmful experiences in disclosure to every category of healthcare professional: medical, mental health, and spiritual/religious. The harm took the form of the professionals responding in ways that are not substantiated by current literature: failing to recognize and identify the NDE as an NDE, denying the possibility that the experience might have been objectively real, diagnosing the NDEr with a mental disorder, and/or demonizing the experience or experiencer. Reports of harm increased with disclosure that was soon after the experience itself and with deeper NDEs. Despite the availability of substantial research-based information about NDEs over the past three decades (Holden, Greyson, & James, 2009), the frequency of harmful disclosure experiences has not diminished for NDEs occurring over the past 80 years (Holden et al., 2014).

Through a growing literature, health professionals are pointing the way to the most therapeutic ways to respond when a client (or anyone) discloses a transpersonal experience (Foster et al., 2009). I have summarized these recommendations using the acronym for near-death experiences: NDEs. The "D" represents "don'ts", that is, responses to avoid; the "N" represents "do's," that is, responses to *enact*; and the "E" represents the likely effects on the experiencer when the respondent has enacted the Ns (Hastings, 1986; Holden, 2015).

- Don't *disregard* the report or *discourage* the experiencer from talking about the experience. Instead, *invite* the experiencer to discuss the experience so as to feel *encouraged* to process the experience out loud—either with you or with someone else you consider more appropriate or qualified.

- Don't *deny* that the experience is a phenomenon that professionals have acknowledged and labeled. Instead, become *knowledgeable* about such experiences so as to be able to recognize and *name* the experience and to thereby *educate* the experiencer about the established category to which the experience belongs.

- Don't *determine* the meaning of the experience for the experiencer. Rather, *inquire* into the evolving meaning the experiencer attributes so he or she approaches the experience consistently from an *exploratory* stance.

- Don't *disbelieve* that the experience is subjectively—and perhaps even objectively—real. Rather, convey that research shows such experiences to be *natural* phenomena that are at least subjectively real, so the experiencer feels *endorsed* as having had a legitimate experience—whatever the experiencer discovers about its correspondence to consensus reality.

- Don't *diagnose* the experience or experiencer based solely on the report of the experience. Instead, *normalize* the experience as something that people throughout history and across cultures have reported to help the experiencer feel *equalized* regarding his or her mental health, at least with regard to the experience itself. In addition, *investigate* the experiencer's condition with regard to spiritual emergency—using Kason's (2008) criteria previously cited—so the experiencer feels *evaluated* with regard to his or her biopsychosociospiritual needs and how best to meet them.

- Don't *demonize* the experience as in some way evil or inherently destructive. Rather, *numinize* the experience—that is, convey that the experience may hold potential for the experiencer to develop spiritually—for example, toward a greater sense of connectedness and/or compassion. Even predominantly distressing experiences appear to hold this potential (Bush, 2009; Rommer, 2000). In this way, the experiencer may be *enlightened* about the psychospiritual developmental, or even transformational, potential that the experience may hold.

- Finally, don't *deprive* the experiencer of resources with which to further process the experience. Instead, *navigate* the experiencer toward such resources, such as print materials and organizations you have vetted for their appropriateness and quality. Offering such options will *equip* the experiencer to find information and support beyond the resources that each of you can provide alone or in your work together.

- For the counselor working long-term with a client to integrate, and possibly more deeply explore and utilize, transpersonal experiences, a foundation for such work is a thorough knowledge of transpersonal experiences (Holden et al., 2014; Kason, 2008). In addition, it is helpful, if not vital, for the counselor to be identified with and operating from a guiding theory of counseling that explicitly addresses transpersonal phenomena, such as the Analytical Psychology of Carl Jung (Stevens, 2001), Roberto Assagioli's (1965) psychosynthesis, or Ken Wilber's (1999) Integral theory.

Assessment issues include determining whether a client is manifesting the "kinder, gentler," more gradual and manageable process of spiritual emergence or the more challenging process of spiritual emergency that involves significant distress and/or dysfunction; in the latter case issues also can include differential diagnosis of spiritual emergency from mental disorder (Bragdon, 2013; Lucas, 2011). Several authors, some representing specific theoretical perspectives and others not, have offered strategies for working with clients with transpersonal experiences (cf., Assagioli, 1965; Bragdon, 1998, 1990; Brown, 1983; Ferrucci, 2009; Foster et al., 2009; Grof & Grof, 1989; Holden et al., 1999; Lucas, 2011). At different times, this work might call for psychoeducation, reformulation of distorted beliefs, exploration of existential concerns such as impact of the experience on relationships and/or life goals, and/or the regulation of further transpersonal experiences through facilitating or reducing them. Though such work might predominantly occur through the modality of individual counseling, the modalities of couple, family, and/or group counseling may be helpful or indicated. Although a thorough treatment of the topic of long-term counseling of clients with transpersonal experiences is beyond the scope of this chapter, the ultimate goal of such work is to assist experiencers in assimilating or accommodating their experiences into coherent worldviews of themselves and the universe and in realizing the full psychospiritual developmental potential of their experiences.

Suggested Resources

Print

Assagioli, R. (1965). *Psychosynthesis: A collection of basic writings.* New York, NY: Penguin.

Holden, J. M. (2015). *Responding to near-death experiencers and other potentially spiritually transformative experiences: Recommendations for healthcare providers* [PDF document]. Available at http://www.coe.unt .edu/sites/default/files/22/129/14_NDE_Acronym_Handout.pdf

Holden, J. M., VanPelt, P. T., & Warren, S. (1999). Spiritual emergency: An introduction and case example. *Counseling and Values, 43,* 163–177.

Kason, Y. (2008). *Farther shores: Exploring how near-death, kundalini, and mystical experiences can transform ordinary lives.* Bloomington, IN: iUniverse.

Lucas, C. G. (2011). *In case of spiritual emergency: Moving successfully through your awakening.* Findhorn, Scotland, UK: Findhorn Press.

Stevens, A. (2001). *Jung: A very short introduction.* New York, NY: Oxford University Press.

Wilber, K. (1999). Integral psychology. In K. Wilber (Ed.), *The collected works of Ken Wilber* (Vol. 4, pp. 423–717). Boston, MA: Shambhala.

Online

American Center for the Integration of Spiritually Transformative Experiences (ACISTE [pronounced "assist"]): https://aciste.org/. This organization holds an annual conference and certifies mental health counselors, spiritual guidance counselors, and life and spiritual coaches in the practice of assisting clients in integrating experiences with the potential for spiritual transformation. The "ACMHP" after author Jan Holden's name stands for "ACISTE Certified Mental Health Professional."

References

Beauregard. M. (2012). *Brain wars: The scientific battle over the existence of the mind and the proof that will change the way we live.* New York, NY: HarperCollins.

Bragdon, E. (2013). *The call of spiritual emergency: From personal crisis to personal transformation* (Rev. 2nd ed.). Woodstock, VT: Lightening Up Press.

Brown, M. Y. (1983). *The unfolding self: Psychosynthesis and counseling.* Los Angeles, CA: Psychosynthesis Press.

Bush, N. E. (2009). Distressing Western near-death experiences: Finding a way through the abyss. In J. M. Holden, B. Greyson, & D. James (Eds.), *The handbook of near-death experiences: Thirty years of investigation* (pp. 63–86). Santa Barbara, CA: Praeger/ABC-CLIO.

Cardeña, E., Lynn, S. J., & Krippner, S. (Eds.). (2000). *Varieties of anomalous experience: Examining the scientific evidence.* Washington, DC: American Psychological Association.

Fall, K., Holden, J. M., & Marquis, A. (2010). *Theoretical models of counseling and psychotherapy* (2nd ed.). New York, NY: Brunner/Routledge.

Ferrucci, P. (2009). *What we may be: Techniques for psychological and spiritual growth through psychosynthesis.* Los Angeles, CA: Jeremy P. Tarcher.

Foster, R. D., & Holden, J. M. (2010). Human and spiritual development and transformation. In C. S. Cashwell & J. S. Young (Eds.). *Integrating spirituality and religion into counseling: A guide to competent practice* (pp. 97–118). Alexandria, VA: American Counseling Association.

Foster, R. D., James, D., & Holden, J. M. (2009). Practical applications of near-death experiences research. In J. M. Holden, B. Greyson, & D. James (Eds.), *The handbook of near-death experiences: Thirty years of investigation* (pp. 235–258). Santa Barbara, CA: Praeger/ABC-CLIO.

Greyson, B. (2010). Seeing dead people not known to have died: "Peak in Darien" experiences. *Anthropology & Humanism, 35*(2), 159–171. doi:10.1111/j.1548–1409.2010.01064.x

Grof, S. (1976). *Realms of the human unconscious: Observations from LSD research.* New York, NY: E. P. Dutton.

Grof, S. (1985). *Beyond the brain: Birth, death, and transcendence in psychotherapy.* Albany, NY: State University of New York Press.

Grof, S., & Grof, C. (Eds.). (1989). *Spiritual emergency: When personal transformation becomes a crisis.* Los Angeles, CA: Jeremy P. Tarcher.

Hastings, A. (1986). A counseling approach to parapsychological experience. *ReVISION, 8*(2), 61–73.

Holden, J. M. (2013). After-math: Counting the aftereffects of spiritually transformative experiences. *Journal of Near-Death Studies, 31*(2), 65–78.

Holden, J. M., Greyson, B., & James, D. (Eds.). (2009). *The handbook of near-death experiences: Thirty years of investigation.* Santa Barbara, CA: Praeger/ABC-CLIO.

Holden, J. M., Kinsey, L., & Moore, T. R. (2014). Disclosing near-death experiences to professional healthcare providers and non-professionals. *Spirituality in Clinical Practice, 1*(4), 278–287. doi:10.1037/scp0000039

James, W. (1990). *The varieties of religious experience.* New York, NY: Random House (Original work published 1902).

Kellehear, A. (2009). Census of non-Western near-death experiences in 2005: Observations and critical reflections. In J. M. Holden, B. Greyson, & D. James (Eds.), *The handbook of near-death experiences: Thirty years of investigation* (pp. 135–158). Santa Barbara, CA: Praeger/ABC-CLIO.

Noble, K. D. (1987). Psychological health and the experience of transcendence. *Counseling Psychologist, 15*(4), 601–614.

Noyes, R., Fenwick, P., Holden, J. M., & Christian, R. (2009). Aftereffects of pleasurable Western adult near-death experiences. In J. M. Holden, B. Greyson, & D. James (Eds.), *The handbook of near-death experiences: Thirty years of investigation* (pp. 41–62). Santa Barbara, CA: Praeger/ABC-CLIO.

Powell, D. H. (2009). *The ESP enigma: The scientific case for psychic phenomena.* New York, NY: Walker.

Radin, D. (1997). *The conscious universe: The scientific truth of psychic phenomena.* New York, NY: HarperCollins.

Radin, D. (2006). *Entangled minds: Extrasensory experience in a quantum reality.* New York, NY: Paraview.

Rommer, B. (2000) *Blessing in disguise: Another side of the near-death experience.* St. Paul, MN: Llewellyn.

Sartori, P. (2004). A prospective study of NDEs in an intensive therapy unit. *Christian Parapsychologist, 16*(2), 34–40.

Streit-Horn, J. (2011). *A systematic review of research on after-death communication (ADC)* (Unpublished doctoral dissertation). University of North Texas, Denton, TX.

Targ, R. (2012). *The reality of ESP: A physicist's proof of psychic abilities.* Wheaton, IL: Quest Books.

Tart, C. T. (2009). *The end of materialism: How evidence of the paranormal is bringing science and spirit together.* Oakland, CA: New Harbinger.

White, R. A. (2001). *Exceptional human experiences: A brief overview.* Retrieved from http://www.ehe.org/display/ehe-page53e5.html?ID=5

Yoga

Tammy H. Cashwell

*Men do not know themselves
and have not learned to
distinguish the different parts
of their being; for these are
usually lumped together by
them as mind. Yoga helps us
to become conscious of the
great complexity of our nature,
and the different forces that move it.*

—Sri Aurobindo

Yoga is a way of life that has been practiced for over 5,000 years. It is neither a philosophy, nor an art, nor a science; rather, it is all three. It is considered a path of enlightenment that can lead to physical, mental, emotional, and spiritual development. The word *yoga* comes from the Sanskrit word *yuj* that carries a double connotation: to join and to come under strict training (Smith, 1991). Therefore, yoga is a type of preparation, with the purpose of joining the individual self with the universal self, thus integrating every aspect of one's being (Sharma & Singh, 2000). Another vital aspect of yoga is its focus on the life energy otherwise known as ch'i, or the chakra system of seven energy centers located along the body from the base of the trunk to the crown of the head. One goal of yoga is to balance this energy in order to balance mind, body, and environment. Ch'i is a Taoist concept that means breath or vital energy. The chakra system is an Eastern concept whereby the energy centers correspond to specific emotions and to particular colors. Yoga helps to keep the energy flowing through the chakras in order to keep the self in balance (Corliss, 2001; Ives & Sosnoff, 2000; Smith, 1991).

The most common type of yoga currently practiced in the Western world is *hatha* yoga. There are eight major variations of hatha yoga. Many of these forms emphasize some combination of physical poses—*asanas;* conscious breathing—*pranayama;* and meditation—*dhyana* (Sharma & Singh, 2000). *Iyengar* and *Kundalini* are both advisable for beginners. Whereas Iyengar focuses on body alignment and joint movement, Kundalini incorporates pranayama, chanting, and dhyana with stretching poses. A third form, *Kripalu,* combines the asanas and psychological element into a type of dhyana. *Viniyoga* is tailored to the needs of each student and focuses on asanas, prayanama, and the spine. Iyengar, Kundalini, Kripalu, and Viniyoga are considered easier forms of hatha yoga. A more difficult form is called *Sivananda;* it not only incorporates the asanas, prayanama, and relaxation, but also involves a vegetarian diet and scripture study. The most challenging types of hatha yoga are *Ashtanga, Jivamukti,* and *Bikram* or *Choudhury.* Ashtanga is also referred to as power yoga because of the emphasis on power, endurance, and flexibility in the asanas while focusing on prayamana. Jivamukti is a type of Ashtanga that also incorporates spiritual practices such as chanting, dhyana, and various readings. Bikram or Choudhury is also referred to as hot yoga because it is performed in rooms that are 100 degrees Fahrenheit or more. Twenty-six asanas are performed in a specific order to help the body stretch even further (Corliss, 2001). Although many Americans view hatha yoga primarily as a form of exercise, it began as much more than that.

Even in hatha yoga, goals for people of the West and for people of India were and are different. For the most part, Westerners are most concerned with power and attractiveness, whereas people of Indian descent seek accuracy and control over all bodily functions.

In the beginning, hatha yoga was performed as groundwork for spiritual yoga. In Hinduism, there are four yogas or paths that can lead to spiritual enlightenment. The first path is called *jnana yoga,* the path through knowledge. The person who chooses this path has an affinity toward cognitions. This knowledge is achieved by first learning, then thinking, and finally to thinking of one's self as Spirit. The second path is called *bhakti yoga,* the path through love. The person who chooses this path has an affinity for emotions. The goal of this path is to love God with all of one's being. This love is achieved through constant prayer, realization that the nuances of love differ depending on the relationship and that these modes may all be applicable in loving God, and finding one's own best form to picture God when worshipping God. The third path is called *karma yoga,* the path through work. The person who chooses this path has an affinity for actions. Karma yoga can be practiced in the form of jnana or bhakti, either of which acts as the purpose behind the works. The final path is called *raja yoga,* the path through psychophysical research. The person who chooses this path has an affinity for science. The experiments follow an eight-step process and are performed on the self to permeate the many layers of the self. Because people are multifaceted, no person is confined to just one path. Journeys on each of the paths are encouraged (Smith, 1991).

Although the history of yoga has many gaps in it, the first signs of yoga date back to the beginning of civilization—approximately 5,000 years ago. A type of Stone Age shamanism, its main goal was to transcend the human condition. Yoga became officially well-known around 3,000 B.C.E. in Indus-Sarasvati (History of Yoga, 2003).

Around this time, the *Vedas* were introduced. The Vedas are ancient texts containing hymns, scriptures, and teachings. The *Rig Veda* is the most sacred text and the primary source of Hinduism. The three main tenets of the Rig Veda are contemplation, higher vision, and ideal harmony (History of Yoga, 2003).

The Pre-Classical Yoga era was from approximately 1800–1500 B.C.E. Gnostic texts called the *Upanishads* were revealed during this time. The Upanishads expanded upon the Vedas. During this time, Buddhism began to surface and emphasized meditation over physical postures—asanas. However, the yoga sages continued to see the benefits of the physical postures. Siddhartha Gautama was one of the first Buddhists to study yoga. The Bhagavad-Gita was also introduced during this era. This was the first scripture devoted entirely to yoga and the first to combine the various yoga practices (History of Yoga, 2003).

The Classical Yoga era followed the Pre-Classical era. During this time Indian author Patanjali wrote the *Yoga-Sutra* to help bring some order to the many different forms of yoga. The *Yoga-Sutra* was distinct in two ways: an emphasis on the study of sacred scriptures and the idea that in order to achieve absolute purity, one must separate body and spirit. This mindset was quite different from the Veda and Pre-Classical Yoga, in that both of these earlier forms stressed the unification of body and spirit. For a period of time, yogis neglected the asanas and focused on meditation until alchemy—a precursor to chemistry—became a force within the world. It was at this point that yogis once again viewed the body as a temple and tried to demonstrate that asanas could actually change the chemistry of the body (History of Yoga, 2003).

The Post-Classical era followed the Classical Yoga era. During this era many branches of yoga emerged, such as hatha and tantra. Rather than focusing on transcendence, these types of yoga focus on accepting and living in the present moment. Beginning in the 1800s, modern yoga was introduced into the United States. Some of the better-known teachers were Yogananda, Krishnamurti, and Maharishi Mahesh Yogi (History of Yoga, 2003).

Today yoga encompasses many languages, such as Hindi, Tibetan, and Sanskrit; crosses many cultures, including Hinduism, Buddhism, Jainism, and Western culture; and is the most varied spiritual practice in the world. It combines asanas—physical postures, pranayama—breathing—and meditation to extend the message of peace (History of Yoga, 2003).

In addition to its message of peace, some research has been conducted to assess the benefits of practicing yoga on a regular basis. Physiological, psychological, and biochemical benefits have been observed. These benefits were cited as the result of yoga practice that combined asana, pranayama, and meditation. Some physiological effects included a decrease in pulse rate, improved respiratory rate and blood pressure; lower levels of reported pain; an increase in brain wave activity, endurance, strength, respiratory efficiency, energy, flexibility, and immunity; normalization of gastrointestinal functions, weight, endocrine functions, and autonomic nervous system functions; and improvements in sleep, excretory processes, and posture. Psychological benefits included: improvement in mood, self-acceptance, social adjustment, attention, memory, and learning efficiency; and a decrease in anxiety, depression, and hostility. Finally, biochemical findings indicated a decrease in glucose, sodium, cholesterol, and total white blood cell count and an increase in hemoglobin, lymphocyte, and Vitamin C (Feuerstein, 2001).

Although some claims are not supported by clinical evidence, a number of authors and researchers have addressed the effects of yoga on various populations and conditions. For example, the *Yoga Studies Newsletter* contains articles pertaining to the effects of yoga on pain, mental health, stroke, fibromyalgia, trauma, body image, infants, cancer, burns, osteoporosis, asthma, and arthritis (*Yoga Studies Newsletter*,

2002–2004). There is clinical evidence to indicate that yoga has a positive effect on flexibility, hypertension, ventilation, stress, mood, muscle strength, carpal tunnel syndrome, rheumatoid arthritis, and asthmas symptoms, and that it can be beneficial for persons with cardiovascular disease (Ives & Sosnoff, 2000).

As evidenced by the previous paragraph, most people can participate in yoga. However, there are some caveats. Anyone with any type of health condition should first consult one's physician before beginning yoga practice and then, upon beginning, should inform the yoga teacher. Although most asanas can be modified, there are precautions for doing certain asanas for people with specific conditions. Some of these conditions include, but are not limited to, joint problems, pregnancy, glaucoma or other eye conditions, recent surgery, and cardiovascular or blood pressure conditions (Lindsay, n.d.; Nespor, 2000).

Although yoga by its very nature is not competitive, Western society tends toward competitiveness. The original lifestyle of the yoga priests was one that was protected, took place in a tropical climate, and embraced vegetarianism—a lifestyle very different from that of most Westerners. Therefore, it is important to emphasize that each person should proceed at one's own pace and comfort level while remaining careful not to strain or perform overly uncomfortable positions (Dworkin, n.d.). With Bikram or Choudhury yoga, it is important to guard against dehydration and heat illnesses because of the extreme temperatures in which the yoga is performed (Funk, 2001). Overall, when done in the right spirit, yoga can be a fulfilling undertaking for many people.

From its ancient beginnings to its modern form, yoga continues to focus on unification through asanas, pranayama, and dhyana. The journey taken depends on the individual, and yoga offers many paths. Yoga is a holistic way to balance body, mind, and spirit.

Suggested Resources

Print

Mesko, S. (2000). *Healing mudras: Yoga for your hands.* New York, NY: Ballantine Wellspring.

Yee, R., & Zolotow, N. (2002). *Yoga: The poetry of the body.* New York, NY: Thomas Dunne.

References

Corliss, R. (2001, April 23). The power of yoga. *Time, 157.* Retrieved from http://content.time.com/time/health/article/0,8599,106356,00.html

Dworkin, S. (n.d.). *A brief history of yoga.* Retrieved from http://www.extensionyoga.com/History.htm

Feuerstein, T. L. (2001). Health benefits of yoga. *Yoga World, 16.* Retrieved from http://www.iayt.org/benefits.html

Funk, L. (2001, April–June). "Hot" yoga: Physiological concerns while exercising in the heat. *Yoga World Newsletter.* Retrieved from http://www.iayt.org.hotyoga.html

History of yoga. (2003). Retrieved from http://www.abc-of-yoga.com/beginnersguide/yogahistory.asp

Ives, J. C., & Sosnoff, J. (2000). Beyond the mind-body exercise hype. *The Physician and Sports Medicine, 28,* 67–81.

Lindsay, J. (n.d.). *Cautions and contraindications.* Retrieved from http://www.jamielindsay.com/cautions.html

Nespor, K. (2000). *Yoga and health: A course for Swedish Yoga teachers, Hruba Skala.* Retrieved from http://www.geocities.com/health_yoga_poetry/phys.html

Sharma, S. K., & Singh, B. (2000). *Yoga: A guide to healthy living.* New York, NY: Barnes & Noble.

Smith, H. (1991). *The world's religions.* San Francisco, CA: Harper.

Yoga Studies Newsletter (2002, January–2004, April). Retrieved from http://www.iayt.org/newsletter.html

About the Editors

Ryan D. Foster, PhD, LPC-S (TX), LPC (VA), NCC, CHST, is assistant professor and clinic coordinator in the Department of Counseling at Tarleton State University in Waco, Texas. During much of his work on the chapters in this volume, Dr. Foster was assistant professor in the Department of Counseling at Marymount University in Arlington, Virginia. His scholarly interests include the use of spiritual and transpersonal experiences in bereavement counseling. In addition, he has published on ethics in counselor education and humanistic sandtray therapy. He has served as a board member of the Association for Spiritual, Ethical, and Religious Values in Counseling, as assistant editor for the *Journal of Near-Death Studies*, and as an editorial review board member for *Counseling and Values*. Correspondence regarding this collection should be sent to Dr. Foster at email: rdfoster@tarleton.edu.

Janice Miner Holden, EdD, LPC-S, LMFT, NCC, ACMHP, is professor and chair of the Department of Counseling and Higher Education at the University of North Texas in Denton, Texas. During 20 years as a counselor educator, Dr. Holden has focused her scholarly pursuits on the transpersonal perspective in counseling: the perspective that includes transpersonal experiences—those transcending the usual personal limits of space and/or time—and transpersonal development—functioning at levels that both include and transcend a sense of personal, individual identity. In particular, she has researched near-death experiences—the counseling needs of experiencers and what these experiences have to reveal about the nature of consciousness and meaning of life. She has served as president of the International Association for Near-Death Studies and as editor of the organization's scholarly peer-reviewed *Journal of Near-Death Studies*. Correspondence regarding her chapters should be sent to Dr. Holden at email: jan.holden@unt.edu.

About the Authors

R. Lewis Bozard, Jr., PhD, MDiv, NCC, LPC, is a counselor in private practice at Peace Counseling & Wellness in Columbia, SC. He is a long-time runner who studied sport and exercise psychology while earning his PhD in Counseling and Counselor Education from the University of North Carolina at Greensboro. He earned his MDiv from Duke University. Correspondence regarding this chapter should be sent to Dr. Bozard at email: lewis.bozard@gmail.com.

Dale Brotherton, PhD, is professor and head of the Department of Human Services at Western Carolina University. Correspondence regarding his monograph should be sent to coauthor Dr. Garrett at email: tlanusta@gmail.com.

Craig S. Cashwell, PhD, is a professor at the University of North Carolina at Greensboro. He has served ASERVIC in a number ways, including as president and editor of *Counseling and Values Journal*. Correspondence regarding his monographs should be sent to Dr. Cashwell at email: cscashwe@uncg.edu.

Tammy H. Cashwell, PhD, LPC, NCC, is an assistant teaching professor in the Department of Counseling at Wake Forest University in Winston-Salem, North Carolina. She received her master's degree in school counseling in 1996 and her doctoral degree in counselor education in 2000 from Mississippi State University. She has experience as a school counselor at both the elementary and high school levels and as a counselor in both a college counseling clinic and a mental health agency. Correspondence regarding her chapter should be sent to Dr. Cashwell at email: cashweth@wfu.edu.

Christopher Faiver, PhD, is professor emeritus of counselor education at John Carroll University in Cleveland, Ohio. A member of Phi Beta Kappa and former ASERVIC Board member, Dr. Faiver is an author or coauthor of numerous articles and two books. Correspondence regarding this chapter should be sent to Dr. Faiver at email: faiver@jcu.edu.

Jennifer M. Foster, PhD, LMHC (FL), joined the faculty at Western Michigan University in the fall of 2012 as an assistant professor in Counselor Education and Counseling Psychology. Before joining WMU, Dr. Foster worked as a licensed mental health counselor as well as professional school counselor in the state of Florida, specializing in childhood trauma. Correspondence regarding this chapter should be sent to Dr. Foster at email: Jennifer.Foster@wmich.edu.

Carol A. Fournier, MA, MS, LCMHC, NCC, is assistant professor retired at The University of Vermont (UVM) and a licensed mental health counselor in private practice in Vermont. She is the founder and director of the Silver Dove Institute, a 501(c3) non-profit (http://www.silverdoveinstitute.org), training spiritually oriented counselors, spiritual directors, and transformational leaders. The Silver Dove Institute is recognized for its contributions to the field of multi-faith spiritual direction by Spiritual Directors International (http://www.sdiworld.org). Carol is an emerita member of the ASERVIC Board of Directors, serving on the Ethics Committee of the Association during the 2005 revision of the ACA *Code of Ethics*. Correspondence regarding her chapter should be sent to Ms. Fournier at email: Carol.Fournier@uvm.edu.

J. T. Garrett, PhD, Eastern Band of the Cherokee Nation, is former director of Public Health and Human Services for the Eastern Band of Cherokee Indians in Cherokee, North Carolina. Correspondence regarding his chapter should be sent to coauthor Dr. Michael Garrett at email: tlanusta@gmail.com.

Michael Tlanusta Garrett, PhD, Eastern Band of the Cherokee Nation, is a school counseling director and professional school counselor with Broward County Public Schools. As author and coauthor of more than 90 professional publications dealing with multiculturalism and social justice, group work, wellness and spirituality, school counseling, working with youth, and counseling Native Americans, Dr. Garrett has written the books, *Walking on the Wind: Cherokee Teachings for Harmony and Balance* (1998), *Native American Faith in America* (2003, 1st ed., and 2012, 2nd ed.), *Counseling and Diversity: Counseling Native Americans* (2011), and edited the book, *Youth and Adversity* (2014).

In addition he has coauthored the books, *Medicine of the Cherokee: The Way of Right Relationship* (1996), *Cherokee Full Circle: A Practical Guide to Ceremonies and Traditions* (2002), and *Counseling and Diversity* (2012). As a Native person who grew up on the reservation in western North Carolina where he still has strong family and community ties, Dr. Garrett's experience with Native people, both professionally and personally, lends a unique perspective and expertise with Native American issues and concerns. Correspondence regarding his chapter should be addressed to Dr. Garrett at email: tlanusta@gmail.com.

Cliff Hamrick, MS, MA, LCDC, LPC-S, is a counselor in private practice at Havamal Therapy in Austin, Texas, where he works with adult men dealing with a variety of issues including depression, anxiety, substance abuse, and past trauma. Cliff is an Ásatrúar, shamanic practitioner, and an active member in the Pagan community of Austin, Texas. Correspondence regarding his chapter should be sent to Mr. Hamrick at email: Cliff.hamrick.lpc@hotmail.com.

Michele L. Kielty, PhD, LPC, is professor of counseling in the Department of Graduate Psychology at James Madison University. Dr. Kielty's main areas of interest are spirituality as related to gender and integrative health and well-being. She has served as president of the Association for Spiritual, Ethical, and Religious Values in Counseling, a division of the American Counseling Association. Correspondence regarding this chapter should be sent to Dr. Kielty at kieltyml@jmu.edu.

Peggy Lesniewicz, PhD, LPCC-S, has been a mental health counselor for 23 years and a hypnotherapist for 10 years. She has recently retired from counseling. Dr. Lesniewicz is a part-time instructor in the Mental Health and School Counseling program at Bowling Green State University in Bowling Green, Ohio. In the past she presented professional workshops on the counseling needs of persons who have had close-to-death and near-death experiences as well as on spirituality and religion in counseling, spiritual emergency, and spirituality and ethics in counseling. Correspondence regarding her chapter should be sent to plesnie@bgsu.edu.

Jo Miller, PhD, is a retired counselor who provided clinical services in Mississippi for many years. Jo is a Reiki and Chinese medicine practitioner and teacher. Correspondence regarding her chapter should be sent to her coauthor Dr. Young at email: jsyoung3@uncg.edu.

Mark Parrish, PhD, is Associate Professor of Counselor Education and College Student Affairs and Chair of the Department of Clinical and Professional Studies at the University of West Georgia. Correspondence regarding his chapter should be sent to coauthor Dr. Garrett at email: tlanusta@gmail.com.

Tracey E. Robert, PhD, LPC, NCCC, is professor in counselor education and Director of Clinical Training, School of Graduate Education & Allied Professions, Fairfield University, Fairfield, Connecticut; a past president of the Association for Spiritual, Ethical, and Religious Values in Counseling (ASERVIC); and a past president of NARACES. After developing an institute for integrating spirituality into research and curriculum, Robert designed and developed the certificate in integrating spirituality and religion into counseling as an outcome of her research and publications in the field on spirituality and work, spiritual interventions, and spirituality and wellness. She recently edited *Critical Incidents in Integrating Spirituality into Counseling*, an ACA publication. Correspondence regarding this chapter should be sent to Dr. Robert at email: trobert@fairfield.edu.

Linda L. Smith, JD, PhD, MA, PC, retired as Associate Dean of the Honors College at the University of Toledo in 2013. A long-time educator and trainer, Dr. Smith now works full-time as a counselor in Toledo, Ohio, on issues related to loss from death, divorce, suicide, illness, and other life changes. Her non-counseling credentials include a law degree and a PhD in English literature, and she has taught courses and workshops dealing with near-death and other death-related experiences, mysticism and spirituality, personality and the grief process, the afterlife and survival of consciousness, and the use of the expressive arts in grief. Dr. Smith is the author of *Annie Dillard*, the critical biography of the Pulitzer Prize–winning mystic. Correspondence regarding her chapter should be sent to Dr. Smith at email: Linda.Smith@utoledo.edu.

Jodi L. Tangen is a doctoral student at the University of North Carolina at Greensboro. Correspondence regarding her chapter should be sent to her coauthor Dr. Cashwell at email: cscashwe@uncg.edu.

Allen H. Weber, PhD, was a Catholic priest who served four years as a counselor in the Counseling Center and 27 years as an associate professor of counselor education at St. Bonaventure University in

St. Bonaventure, New York. From 2000 to 2003, he served as president of ASERVIC, a division of the American Counseling Association. Dr. Weber passed away on December 25, 2015; thus, his contribution to this book was published posthumously. The editors wish to dedicate his chapter in memory of Dr. Weber's presence as a person of faith and his many contributions to the field of counseling. Correspondence regarding his chapter should be sent to editor Dr. Ryan D. Foster at email: rdfoster@tarleton.edu.

Cyrus Williams, PhD, is associate professor in the School of Psychology and Counseling at Regent University. Correspondence regarding his chapter should be sent to coauthor Dr. Garrett at email: tlanusta @gmail.com.

J. Scott Young, PhD, NCC, LPC, is Professor and Chair of the Department of Counseling and Educational Development at the University of North Carolina at Greensboro. He was a professor for 12 years at Mississippi State University and has been a practicing counselor in private practice, agency, and hospital settings for 20 years. His leadership in the field includes service as president of the *Association for Spiritual Ethical and Religious Values in Counseling* and as a member of the Governing Council and Executive Committee for the *American Counseling Association.* He is coeditor of the book *Integrating Spirituality into Counseling: A Guide to Competent Practice* and the text *Counseling Research: Quantitative, Qualitative, and Single Subject Design.* He has published numerous articles on the interface of clinical practice with spirituality and religion. Correspondence regarding his chapter should be sent to Dr. Young at email: jsyoung3@uncg.edu.